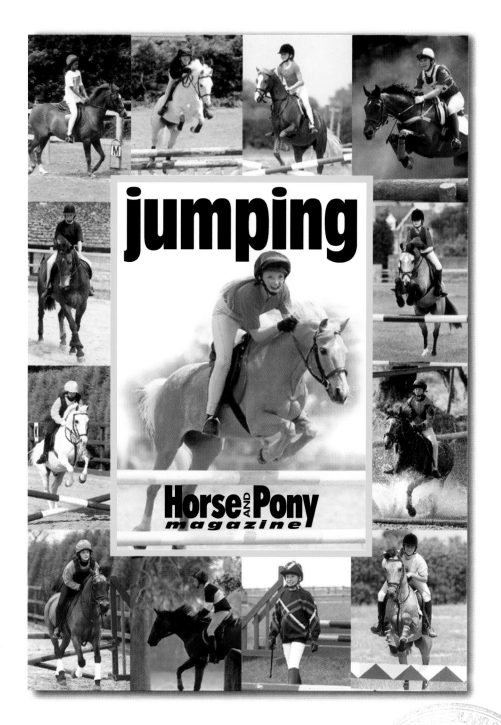

jumping

Horse AND Pony
magazine

Jackie Budd

R

RINGPRESS

contents

RINGPRESS

Ringpress Books
PO Box 8
Lydney
Gloucestershire
United Kingdom
GL15 4YN

Tel
01 594 845577

Fax
01 594 845599

First published
1999
*in association with
Horse and Pony
magazine*

© 1999 Ringpress
Books Ltd
and Jackie Budd

Designer
Lance Bellers

ISBN
1 86054 150 X

Printed and bound in
Singapore

1 2 3 4 5 6 7 8 9 10

*All photographs
courtesy of*

what is jumping?

Ask any young rider what part of riding they enjoy most, and the chances are they will say "Jumping!" Once you have mastered the skill of jumping, a whole new daring world of fun and excitement opens up. Clear round rosettes, show jumping arenas with their brightly-coloured poles, the thrill of galloping cross-country or simply popping over a log out on a ride – there's no doubt jumping is one of the most thrilling challenges you and your pony can take on together.

Step by step to success

If you have yet to tackle any jumping in your riding lessons, you may be feeling a little anxious about the idea. Don't worry – you are not alone! At first, almost every rider has exactly the same worries that may be going through your head. Am I going to be able to control the pony? What if he won't go over the fence? What if I fall off?

Top riders at the big shows make clearing those gigantic fences look easy. Even at a local gymkhana, super-confident riders seem to be whizzing round the jumps on nimble ponies and it all appears simple.

In fact, there are no big or mysterious secrets about jumping. Any rider can do it, and any pony can do it. The key is to learn one step at a time. Give yourself and your pony a chance to practise each lesson thoroughly before trying to move on to something more difficult, and you will be amazed at what you can achieve together.

This book will take you through those stages one by one, giving you lots of ideas on how to work on your new skills, either in your lessons or at home on your own pony. There will be hints on how to deal with any hiccups you might have, too, because, as with anything to do with ponies, there are sure to be a few!

More experienced riders who have done some jumping can learn how to polish up that all-important basic technique, find out how to teach

Jumping fun isn't just about rosettes and arenas!

There's no great mystery about how a pony jumps. Think of it as a large canter stride with extra 'lift'.

a young pony to jump, or clock up more of those clear rounds. Discover how to ride more effectively, so that, instead of always making the winning line-up with a push-button pony, you can get the best out of ponies that are less talented, or more difficult to ride.

Jumping – what's new?

You may be surprised to learn that, if you have got the hang of canter in your lessons, you are already a long way towards being able to jump! Why? Because, when a pony jumps, all he is actually doing is taking a big canter stride that has extra 'lift' in it to allow him to clear the obstacle in his way.

Of course, going over a small fence like a cross-pole requires only a small amount of additional 'pop', making the leap fairly easy for the rider to stay in balance with. In top-class competition (see pic left), horses need to make an extra huge lift, to clear fences that are enormously high and wide. Even so, their movement is based on exactly the same extra-large canter stride your pony uses as he tackles a tiny cross-pole.

a pony's eye view

It takes two to jump! Jumping is about a partnership, between you and the pony you are riding. So, what does he think about the whole business?

How many ponies in the wild do you see leaping over hedges or tree trunks? Do ponies enjoy jumping at all, or is it a completely unnatural thing to ask them to do?

Jumping isn't totally artificial for a pony. Horses are natural athletes, and, as we have said, the jumping action is an extension of the normal canter stride. With his agility, sure footedness and instinctive cunning, a wild horse or pony would certainly have had leaping over a ditch or rocky outcrop in his repertoire of escape skills.

Most horses do seem to enjoy jumping with a rider once they have been shown what to do. However, horses and ponies are also good at saving energy. Generally speaking, they like an easy life. Left to themselves, they would be unlikely

What is your pony thinking about those fences?

to make the effort to jump over an obstacle if going around it was a simpler option.

Remember this whenever you are approaching a jump. To a pony (in particular a youngster), jumping over fences does not make much sense. From a pony perspective, two important signposts point the way to successful jumping, whether the fences are 2ft or 5ft high:

● **The rider must try to make it just as easy, or even easier, for the pony to carry on and jump cleanly over the fence than to grind to a halt, run past it, or knock it down.**
● **The rider must make sure their pony enjoys jumping as much as he/she does.**

Get these right and your pony will be happy to 'do his bit'. The two of you will be well on your way to becoming a winning team.

the *right pony* for jumping

Your riding school should provide an obedient pony to get you started with jumping.

pace you set, pop over it neatly in a straight line and slow down obediently when asked to at the other side.

Whether he belongs to a riding school, a friend, or you are lucky enough to own such an equine angel, a calm and trustworthy pony like this is absolutely essential for learning to jump.

Moving on

Given the right aids (signals) by their rider, ponies of all shapes and sizes are quite athletic enough to clear small fences. But, just as some of your classmates are particularly good at gymnastics and athletics, there are ponies who have a natural talent and flair for jumping.

When you progress beyond the basics and start to work on improving your skills further, or if you want to compete more seriously in jumping competitions, you will want a pony that is ideally suited to the job.

Horses for courses

No doubt you have heard people use the expression 'horses for courses'. Funnily enough, that saying is particularly true when it comes to ponies and jumping.

Any pony is capable of jumping a small fence, as long as he is fit and well and has been trained to jump, so he knows what is expected. But to really enjoy their jumping, riders of different levels of ability are best mounted on different types of pony.

Let's take a look at the sort of characters we are talking about:

Ponies to get started on

When you first begin jumping, there are 101 instructions to remember every time you head for a fence. Steering, speed, looking up, going forwards – the last thing you want to be worrying about is whether your pony actually knows what he is supposed to do when he gets there!

Learner riders must have a pony who knows his job. An experienced, reliable 'school-master' pony will give you all the confidence you need. He won't get too upset about the odd mistake, because he enjoys jumping and knows what it is all about. Give him approximately the right aids and he should approach the jump at the

If you get a flashy jumping pony, you will need the ability to handle him.

Once you get into jumping more seriously, you may want a pony that has become a 'specialist'.

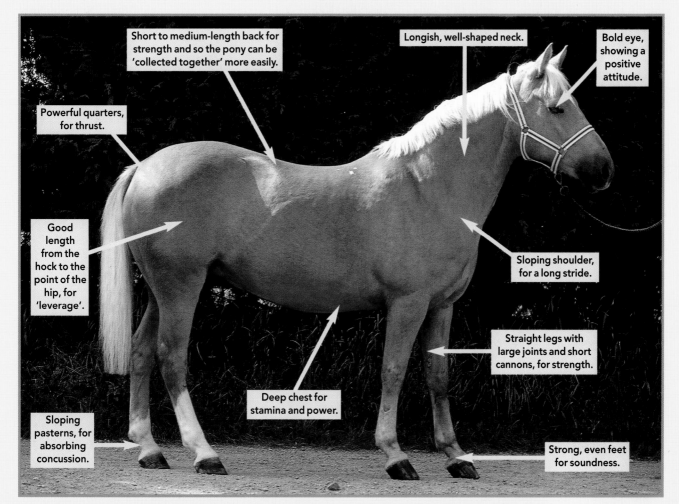

Short to medium-length back for strength and so the pony can be 'collected together' more easily.

Longish, well-shaped neck.

Bold eye, showing a positive attitude.

Powerful quarters, for thrust.

Good length from the hock to the point of the hip, for 'leverage'.

Sloping shoulder, for a long stride.

Straight legs with large joints and short cannons, for strength.

Deep chest for stamina and power.

Sloping pasterns, for absorbing concussion.

Strong, even feet for soundness.

what makes a good jumping pony?

A pony that finds jumping easy and fun will jump well. If you want a pony with a real talent for jumping, keep the following points in mind:

Good conformation

The way a pony is 'put together' can make a big difference to how easy or difficult he finds the job of jumping, once the fences start to get bigger. A jumping pony may be of any breed or mixture of breeding, but he will usually have the points of good conformation shown in the picture above.

Good style

Some ponies instinctively show a good technique over a fence, tucking their front legs up, rounding their backs and whisking their hindlegs out of the way as they go over. Style can be improved by training, but, if a pony is a naturally clever, careful and agile jumper, he has a head start.

Experience

Jumping takes lots of practice, for ponies as well as riders. If you want to do well in classes where the courses are bigger and more complicated, choose an older pony who has experience at the level you are aiming for and can give you confidence. Young ponies who are still learning themselves need expert riders and should be brought on slowly over small fences until they are ready to progress.

Positive attitude

It seems obvious, but a successful jumping pony must love jumping. As long as you ride kindly and correctly, he should be a genuine character who wants to jump for you and is always looking forward to the next fence. A shifty, unreliable pony who is forever looking for a way out is never going to be a winner or give you much fun, even if he can be brilliant when he chooses to be! Some ponies do find jumping round after round boring – these characters need to be given a different job to do that they enjoy more.

Sensible approach

At every show, wild-eyed, madcap ponies can be seen chasing around the arena, heads in the air, their riders barely in control. Sometimes the jumps stay up, but all too often you will find that, as the fences increase in size, these ponies and riders come unstuck and poles go flying. Good teamwork is built on getting the basics right. For that, you need a pony who is steady and sensible enough to listen to his rider and learn the correct way to go. Yes, he must be brave. But he must be careful too, and want to leave the jumps up instead of knocking them flying.

are you ready?

You don't need to be an expert rider to begin jumping, but you must be able to stop, start and steer a pony at walk, trot and canter.

If you are keen and really enjoying your riding, it's tempting to want to get jumping within your first few lessons. But learning anything new always goes more smoothly if you really feel prepared for it and happy about having a go. So, before we dive in to talk about the business of jumping itself, let's get set up for a flying start.

In control?

You don't have to be an expert rider 'on the flat' before you start learning to jump. To be safe and enjoy it, though, you must have progressed in your riding far enough to be able to control an obedient pony confidently. Otherwise you could soon be back down to earth with a bump (literally!) with your confidence taking a real knock.

So far, your instructor will have concentrated on teaching you how to ask your pony to speed up, slow down and change direction. All the time, you have been getting used to the 'feel' of the pony's movement, staying secure in the saddle, and working on giving the aids without losing that balance.

This is called developing an 'independent seat'. It means that, however the pony moves, you are able to stay with him and in control of him without having to grab or hang on to the reins to keep steady.

To be ready for jumping, riders must be able to keep their body still and balanced in the saddle while they give the aids.

Once you are quite happy and confident at trot and canter (not just as part of a group but by yourself, too), you are ready to learn to jump. However, you do need to do more work on your seat 'on the flat' before trying jumping, if:

● You aren't too confident about controlling your pony's speed.

● You haven't got the hang of keeping your pony straight yet.

● You are still worried about keeping your balance.

● You sometimes feel unsteady and have to grab at the reins to stay secure.

● When you use your legs, your whole body tends to move about in the saddle.

A good instructor would never ask you to jump if you were not ready to have a go. Poles on the ground are a safe way of introducing the idea of jumping to riders who aren't quite ready to leave the ground yet.

Whoops!

Like everything else in riding, jumping is about balance. When a pony jumps, the thrusting movement he makes when he takes off can feel quite jerky at first. It takes a lot of practice to be able to stay in balance with your pony as he jumps and lands. Getting the hang of this, and being able to control what he does going up to the fence and away from it on the other side, is quite a skill. Each jump can be different, too – this is the challenge of jumping!

Don't expect to get it right straight away, or every time. There are sure to be more than a few lurching take-offs, wobbly landings and general sticky moments as you try to get the knack of staying with the pony's motion. You may even fall off a few times – even the best riders have had a bucket-load of falls!

Try not to tense up and worry too much about falling off, or it will spoil your fun. Most falls, particularly when you are learning, are not very spectacular. Rather than being sent flying dramatically into the air, you are far more likely to make an undignified slither to the ground, finishing up with no harm done except a pair of dirty jodhs and a red face! Even so, as you will see on the next page, it is best to wear a body protector and approved helmet for jumping, just in case you happen to have a bumpy landing.

Lessons on the lunge are a good way of helping to develop an 'independent seat'.

overcoming *nerves*

Jumping can make even the most confident and experienced rider nervous. Remember that ponies are super-sensitive to any anxiety in their riders, so work on trying to relax and enjoy it, whether you are in your first lesson or about to enter the arena at a show. Here are some tips to help beat those jumping jitters:

● Sing a favourite song (to yourself!) – preferably make it one with a regular beat you can tune in to your pony's stride.

● Picture yourself relaxing on a sunny beach, complete with palm trees and an ice cream!

● Imagine approaching the fence and sailing over it in Olympic gold medal-winning style!

● Sit up tall and take deep breaths, filling your lungs right down to the very bottom, then slowly letting the air out.

● Try to forget about what the other riders in the lesson are up to (or other competitors in the ring) – focus on yourself and what the instructor is saying.

Everyone falls off sometimes! Try not to worry – most falls are not at all dramatic.

before you start

Whoa! We are almost ready to get jumping, but not quite. Safety must always come first in riding, and is especially important in jumping. It's all about being properly prepared.

getting in gear
rider

Having all the right protective gear doesn't mean you are sure to fall off, but if you do, it shouldn't hurt too much! Most of the kit you need you will already be using in your riding lessons. If your instructor says it is time to start jumping, make sure that you have:

- the latest approved standard crash hat.
- gloves.
- proper riding footwear, with a smooth sole and small heel.
- jodhpurs.
- a body protector (see picture, right).

Once you are good enough to enter a show, you will need:

- a show jacket.
- a white shirt and a tie.
- jodhpur boots or long riding boots.

When you are ready to enter shows, you will need a tweed or dark-coloured jacket and matching hat cover.

tip for the top

Avoid plain, smooth leather reins for jumping. Rubber-covered, plaited, laced or 'continental' style reins give much better grip.

Left: Ponies sometimes need to wear a martingale or stronger bit for the excitement of jumping. Don't forget those gloves!

tip for the top

An old stirrup leather makes a good neckstrap. Fit it part-way up the pony's neck so it is easily to hand in case of need!

pony

● At first, it is helpful if the pony wears a neckstrap. This gives something to grab hold of for balance that is not directly attached to the pony's sensitive mouth! Your pony may wear a martingale, which has a built-in neckstrap. Many ponies who do a lot of jumping, particularly at shows, do wear a martingale, as it helps prevent the pony getting his head too high if he gets excited.

● Using safety stirrup irons is a good idea, as they will release your foot if you fall.

● Boots will protect the pony's legs against knocks. Choose between:

Brushing boots *which cover the whole way around the lower leg from below the knee to above the fetlock.*

Tendon boots *which are like brushing boots for the forelegs, but are open at the front and have extra padding at the back.*

Over-reach boots *which are round, bell-shaped rubber boots that go around the pastern in case the pony clips the heel of a forefoot with a back foot as he lands.*

● Most riders begin jumping using an ordinary general-purpose saddle. Do check, however, that the saddle you use allows your knee to come forwards more than normal and your seat to move backwards easily, as it will need to when you take up jumping position.

● Serious jumping fans may want to invest in a special saddle designed for the job. The 'tree' (frame) of a jumping saddle is built so that the flaps are 'forward-cut' and the rider can easily get into the correct position for jumping.

Boots will help protect the pony's legs from knocks. Use brushing (shown) or tendon boots on the lower legs and over-reach boots to protect the heels.

check it out

Two important checks have to be made every time you and your pony are getting ready to do some jumping.

Is your girth tight?
Have a feel of your pony's girth and take it up a hole if necessary. You don't want to finish up on the floor before you even reach the fence! Get into the habit of checking the girth every time you start a jumping session.

Have you shortened your stirrups?
Stirrups are always raised between one and three holes from your normal riding length for jumping. This helps you stay secure in the saddle and adjust your riding position as the pony goes over the fence. You will see how this works over the next few pages.

Always check your girth is tight before a jumping session.

Your stirrups will need to go up several holes.

safety sense

Whenever you are practising jumping (especially at home with your own pony):

● Always wear your safety gear and check your girth and stirrups first.

● Never jump alone.

● Only use safe fences (see pages 42-43).

● Use the correct distances between fences (see pages 22-23).

● Keep fences small.

● Only jump in an enclosed space.

● Check the gate is shut.

● Make sure you have enough room to approach fences correctly.

● Only jump if the ground is suitable, i.e., not if it is too wet and slippery, too hard, or too rough.

● Loosen up your pony and get his attention with some flat-work first.

● Don't overdo jumping and make your pony fed up.

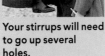
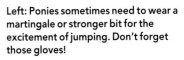

take your position

After all the trouble you have taken over the past weeks or months trying to hang your legs down low and sit tall in the saddle, now it's time to jump, the instructor is going to tell you it's all change!

The rider's position has to be adjusted for jumping to make it easy to stay balanced with the pony throughout the movement over the fence and not to interfere with him.

Why the short stirrups?

When you are riding your pony along on the flat at walk, trot and canter, sitting tall over the centre of balance of his body helps you stay secure. Your bottom (or 'seat') spreads out on the saddle to keep you in place. Having long stirrups helps this happen.

However, as the pony moves on to faster paces and to jump, his centre of balance moves forwards. When he brings his hindlegs underneath him to push off over the fence, it suddenly shifts even further forwards. If the rider stayed in an upright position she would get hopelessly left behind the momentum as the pony took off, making things very difficult and uncomfortable for them both. And, as he flicked up his back end to clear the jump with his hindlegs, the rider would finish up by being catapulted into the air!

What is needed is a position that will help you come forwards with the movement, taking your weight off the pony's back. By shortening the stirrups, you can lift your bottom out of the saddle and secure yourself in a forward position over the pony's centre of balance as he makes a jump.

This different position will feel odd at first, because you will feel much more 'bunched up', with lots more of your thigh and knee in front of you. But that is what will help stop you tipping off balance.

Look carefully at the pictures at the bottom of the page of a rider using jumping position as her pony approaches and goes over a fence. By folding up her body into a kind of concertina, or collapsible W-shape

The long leg and tall body of the position for riding on the flat aims to keep you steady over the pony's centre of balance.

the phases of the jump

Studying the way a pony makes a jump will help you understand why it is so easy to be sent off-balance, and why it is so important to keep in jumping position. There are five main stages of the jump. We will look at how to ride each one in more detail later.

1 approach
As the pony comes up to the jump, he steadies up to get a good look at it. The last stride is a short one, as he gathers himself together. He has to bring his back end underneath his body more so that it can help power his heavy front end off the ground. Just before taking off, he will stretch his head down slightly to weigh up the size and shape of the fence and judge the right place to take off.

2 take off
As he takes off, his head, neck and forelegs come up and forwards.

on its side, she creates angles in her body which can then open out or squash up to go with the pony and let him get on with jumping without any interference. She can pivot on her knee and use the angles of her body as shock-absorbers. Instead of being thrown out of the saddle by the movement, she can remain still and allow the pony to use himself freely.

For jumping, your security and balance in the saddle depends on your weight being supported, not on your bottom and seat-bones, as in the usual riding position, but on your legs and weight in the stirrups.

Above: Keeping an upright position over a fence is uncomfortable for the pony and the rider.

In jumping, squashing up the angles of the hips, knees and ankles helps absorb the movement of the pony's body. This is helped by having shorter stirrups.

Now your weight is supported not by your bottom in the saddle, but your knees and your feet in the stirrups.

a great inventor

If it wasn't for one man, jumping for horses and riders would never have really taken off at all.

Back in the last years of the 1800s, an Italian cavalry officer called Frederico Caprilli became so tired of patching up his officers and horses after falls that he came up with a totally new way of riding across rough country and obstacles. It involved the rider shortening his stirrups to get into a forward position off the horse's back. This gave the horse freedom to stretch its neck and use its body naturally.

Before Caprilli, riders used a long stirrup at all times. Even when tackling fences, they either sat bolt upright as if they were doing high-school work in the manege, or leant right back over a fence hunting-style, hanging on to the horse's mouth to stay put.

Both of these old riding styles were hopeless for jumping. Besides leaving the rider very insecure, they were extremely uncomfortable and restricting for the poor horse. But once everyone caught on to the 'forward seat', it was up, up and away!

3 flight

When the jump is small, there is little time for the 'flight' stage, because almost as soon as the hindfeet are leaving the ground, the forefeet are touching down the other side. But, as the jumps get larger, more time is spent in the air. This is sometimes called the 'moment of suspension'.

To jump in good style, the pony tucks his forelegs up neatly underneath him. He lowers his head and neck and rounds his back to make an arch with his body that is called a 'bascule'. His hindlegs are stretched out and lifted to clear the fence behind.

4 landing

The forelegs touch down first, one at a time, followed by the hindlegs. The pony's head comes up to help re-balance him.

5 get-away

Now the pony gathers himself together again ready to take the next canter stride away from the jump.

sitting pretty

Whenever you watch show jumping or eventing on the television or at a big show, does it always amaze you how those riders sit tight over such huge fences, never interfering with their horses? Of course, these riders have years of experience behind them and we won't be tackling international-sized fences just yet! But even over an 18-inch cross-pole, getting into and keeping a good jumping position is one of the secrets of successful jumping.

Your position can make the difference between you landing in the same spot as your pony, or left behind on the ground! But there is more to it than that. By sitting correctly and being effective in the saddle, the rider can help the pony make the best possible jump. Perfect your jumping position from the start and you will have no problems once the fences start to get bigger.

tip for the top

Imagine the pony underneath you suddenly does a disappearing trick. If you are sitting correctly, you would stay perfectly balanced. If you are tipping forwards from the hips you could find yourself flat on your face!

Top riders are able to stay in a perfectly-balanced jumping position whatever the height of the fences.

position points

Keep your head up, looking ahead – you're still in charge of the steering!

Relax your shoulders, elbows and wrists. As the neck stretches out, the arms move forwards from the shoulder, so the pony can use his head and neck freely.

Keep your back flat. Make sure your shoulders don't tip further forwards than your knees.

Keep a straight line from your elbows to the bit. Avoid leaning on the neck.

Bend from the hips. Think of squatting down.

Push your bottom backwards. It should 'hover' over the saddle.

Have a firm, but not tight, contact on the reins.

Keep your lower leg underneath your body, close to the pony's side.

Rest your weight on the balls of your feet. The heels are slightly down and ankles supple.

flat work first

try this

First practise perfecting your jumping position on the flat. You need to be happy doing this in trot and canter before trying any jumping.

● Shorten your stirrups. Fold into jumping position in halt, with your bottom poised over the saddle. Balance without leaning on the pony's neck. Mind that lower leg doesn't swing back!

● Now try to keep this position at walk and then trot. Focus on absorbing the movement of the trot using your ankles, knees and hips and not relying on the reins. Trying not to stiffen up, wedge your knees into the front of the saddle flap to help balance. Keep those heels down and look up. It's not as easy as it looks, is it?

● When you feel secure, go forwards to canter. Now we're really moving! You will probably find this slightly easier than trot. Remember to keep looking ahead, with your weight down into your heels and lower legs wrapped around the pony's sides directly beneath you, keeping your pony going. Stick that bottom backwards, not upwards!

● Try keeping the position up doing large circles and simple changes of direction. Once you get confident, you can try a 'figure of eight'.

Bending and flexing the hip and ankle joints will make them more supple.

There are lots of chances to give those calf muscles a stretch.

do your homework!

try this

Jumping position can be practised out hacking, or even without a pony! Try these exercises at home. Doing just a few each day will improve your suppleness and you will soon find adjusting your riding position easy.

● Stand with your heels on the floor and your toes resting on a shallow step (such as a hearth), or a heavy book. Stay there for the count of 10 and feel your calf muscles stretching. Try some gentle bends and stretches in that position.

● When you are sitting watching the TV, rotate your ankles round eight times in one direction, then eight times the other way.

● Holding on to the back of a chair lightly for balance, bend at the hips. Keep your head up (but try not to stiffen your neck). Hold this for the count of 10 and then straighten up.

● Holding the chair and keeping your back straight, look ahead and bend at the knees. Your heels need to stay on the floor. Hold this for 10 and then gently straighten up.

● Combine the two exercises above, as if you were going into jumping position on your pony. Notice how your bottom needs to move backwards. Hold this for a few seconds before straightening up. Do this alongside a mirror to see if it looks right.

● Stand up straight. Bring your shoulders up towards your ears, then backwards and down.

Do eight of each exercise. Afterwards, hold each heel up in turn behind your back to let the leg muscles relax again.

Practise keeping jumping position at walk, trot and canter and through bends and circles.

This rider would find it easier if her stirrups went up a hole or two more. Can you see how a shorter length would help her to squash down towards the pony's neck instead of tipping forwards?

tip for the top

Think of squashing down rather than leaning forwards. The only part of you that moves forwards is your arms, which reach towards the mouth to give the pony freedom over the jump. Your bottom goes backwards, NOT upwards. Remember: **squash down - bottom back!**

At home, use the back of a chair to help balance while you go through your suppleness exercises.

polishing up positions

Getting jumping position right is not as easy as it looks. Work at it though – a balanced, secure position can make all the difference between your pony sailing over a fence, grinding to a halt or knocking down a pole just when you thought a clear round was in the bag.

Ponies *can* be cheeky or careless, but as we will find out in the pages to come, most jumping mistakes and mishaps are down to you not doing your stuff right! For example, a pony could approach and take off on a perfect stride, only to drop a leg on a pole or stumble on landing because his rider has interfered with his mouth, or put him off-balance as he was going over.

Most rider faults over the fence come from either the way you use your body or the way you use your hands. When you first start jumping, position faults are often caused by tension, perhaps because you are worried or nervous.

what's wrong here?

problem 1

too upright

This rider may be admiring the view, but sitting as if she is in an armchair is not helping her pony. Look how much extra weight sitting down in the saddle puts on to the hindquarters, preventing him from making a nice, round shape over the fence. The rider is well behind the forward movement too, which will unbalance the pony.

 tip If the rider folded her body from the hips, squashing her chest towards the pony's neck and giving with her hands, he would find jumping much easier. And she would be in much more control.

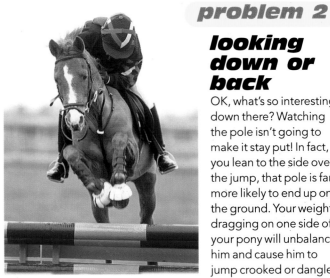

problem 2

looking down or back

OK, what's so interesting down there? Watching the pole isn't going to make it stay put! In fact, if you lean to the side over the jump, that pole is far more likely to end up on the ground. Your weight dragging on one side of your pony will unbalance him and cause him to jump crooked or dangle a leg on that side. Looking down also makes you hunch your back stiffly instead of keeping it flat, close to the pony's neck. What's more, you can't see what's coming up next!

 tip Look up and ahead between the pony's ears all the way up to, over, and away from the fence. Have your shoulders square with the pony's shoulders and this will keep you both in line. Aim for an even length and pressure on both reins and from both of your legs.

problem 3

weight too far forwards

There are several errors in these two photos. Although being too upright, as in Problem 1, causes mistakes, it is just as uncomfortable for a pony if you throw yourself right up his neck. Maybe you are thinking that flinging yourself forwards will help urge him on. No way – look how the pony above is forced to jump flat, risking a knockdown. He is having to get his forelegs up to take off despite having to lift all the rider's weight on his neck as well.

By pushing her hands up the pony's neck and leaning on it, instead of simply bringing the hands forward towards the mouth, the rider is making things even more difficult, as she has lost all contact with the mouth. Throwing the reins at your pony over the jump or dropping them just before it means you have lost your lines of communication.

In the photo to the right, instead of folding from the waist, the rider has tipped forwards on to her knees, which are tight and stiff. As a result, the lower leg often slips back and the toes point down. Bad news – now the rider is likely to land in a real heap, unable to ride an effective get-away.

tip Don't be in a hurry! Wait for the fence to come to you (see pages 28-29). Instead of throwing yourself forwards, think of squashing the angles of your body together and sticking your bottom backwards. This will help keep your legs underneath you. Push your weight down through your heels (check your stirrups are short enough – too long stirrups often cause a rider to tip forwards instead of squashing down into jump position). Keep a steady contact up to and over the fence, letting the pony take your hands forwards as he stretches his neck out.

problem 4

fixing the hands

Fixing the hands may not cause too many problems over small fences, but once the jumps go up or get wider – or if the pony happens to take off on a bad stride – he has to use his head and neck much more to keep in balance.

Unless the rider allows him freedom, the result is a cramped, uncomfortable jump, and probably a pole down.

tip A pony needs 'allowing' hands from his rider, giving him the freedom to use his head and neck for balance. Think of your reins as two lengths of elastic, which you need to keep just a light tension on at all times, giving your pony 'space' but also reassurance that you are still there and all is well.

problem 5

getting left behind

Yikes! Perhaps this pony approached in too much of a rush, or else with not enough energy, taking off on an awkward stride and catching his rider unawares. Or he may have made an extra-huge leap she wasn't expecting. Whatever the reason, she has been badly 'left behind' the movement of the jump because she didn't fold forwards from the hips as the pony left the ground. In this situation there is no avoiding coming down with a bump in the saddle, because you have lost all lower leg control.

tip Try not to anticipate the jump or panic as it approaches, trying to 'see' a stride. If you are worried about getting left behind, it often helps to come into jump position early on the approach so you are ready – but keep your rein contact and don't tip forwards. Aim for a steady approach with rhythmical, even strides and, nine times out of 10, the pony will arrive at a perfectly good place for a smooth take-off. Then all you have to do is fold down into jump position as the pony comes up – but not before. Keep looking up all the time!

If you do ever get left behind, let the reins slip through your fingers rather than hanging on to them for balance. A pony who gets repeatedly caught in the mouth is not going to be happy to keep jumping for long.

problem 6

standing in the stirrups and raising the hands

This rider looks as if she is trying to jump the fence herself instead of letting her pony get on with the job! Far from being encouraging, standing up, raising your hands and sticking your elbows out on take-off only restricts your pony. You are fixing your rein contact,

stiffening your back and legs, and bringing all your weight on to his forehand just as he is trying to lift off into the air!

tip Standing in the stirrups commonly happens when the rider is too anxious (see pages 28-29). Try to relax and let the pony take care of the jump himself. As you feel him come up underneath you, simply squash the angles between your ankles, knees and hips, bring your chest towards his neck and your hands forwards.

practice makes perfect

Don't worry if you recognise some of your own faults here. A good position is about timing and co-ordination. The more jumping you do, the better you will get without even realising it. We can't jump the fences for our ponies. All we can do is work on our riding to give them the best chance of going clear, and having fun.

Ground poles help both ponies and riders to learn about balance and rhythm.

first steps

Once you are feeling steady in jumping position, it's time to get out some poles! Riding over poles laid out on the ground is a basic exercise for preparing any pony and rider for jumping. It is used for teaching young horses and ponies how to jump as well as getting riders used to the feeling of jumping. Never think this is just for beginners, though! Even the best, most experienced partnerships regularly use simple poles on the ground in their training.

How do poles help?
Why bother with poles on the ground – why not just get on with jumping 'real' fences? Pole exercises are helpful because:

The RIDER is learning to:
● Think about her speed.
● Feel the little 'hop' a pony makes over a jump.
● Stay in balance.
● Keep up a rhythm towards a fence.
● Steer straight.

The PONY is learning to:
● Accept going forwards over an obstacle.
● Think where he is putting his feet!

● Co-ordinate his legs and move in a nice rhythm.
● Go in a straight line.
● Loosen his back and strengthen the right muscles for jumping.

Poles apart
Poles can be laid out on the ground singly, set out parallel to each other in a line, or placed on a curve or circle. In a lesson, your instructor will make sure the poles are always the correct distance apart so the ponies step cleanly over them rather than tripping up. Every rider should know what this distance is, however, so they can get it correct when practising at home.

For walking only:
2 1/2ft-3 ft (0.8-1m)

For trotting only:
4 ft-4 1/2 ft (1.2-1.3m)

For trotting or cantering over:
7ft-8ft (2.1-2.6m)

The exact distance will depend on the individual pony's size and length of stride. These figures are for *ponies* – horses take longer strides and so would need a little more space between each pole.

Get the feel of pole-work by riding over single poles set out randomly around the school or paddock.

Learn how to measure how far apart the poles have to be placed.

pole practice

Build pole exercises step by step
● Before setting off down a line of poles, get the feel by walking over single poles laid out at all sorts of angles around the field or manege. Aim for the centre of each and plan to step over cleanly in the middle of the pony's stride. When you are happy, try this in trot. Look and think where you are going!

● Your instructor will probably set out a line of poles next, starting with three and gradually increasing the number. Tackle the line first in walk, then trot.

pole points

● Approach in a straight line, aiming for the centre.
● In trot, rise, or take your weight slightly off the saddle (you do not need to fold right down into jumping position).
● Keep looking up where you are going.
● Keep your legs on the pony's sides. If you feel him slowing up, give little squeezes with your heels to encourage him on. Try not to lose your balance.
● You will feel the bounce-bounce-bounce as your pony picks his feet up higher over the poles. Push your heels down and try to absorb this in your legs.
● The pony may seem to want to stretch his neck a little more, so allow your hands slightly forwards. Keep just a light, even contact on the reins. Try not to lean on to his neck.
● If you feel yourself getting unsteady, grab a chunk of mane or the neckstrap. Don't snatch at the reins or thump back down into the saddle.
● Aim to keep up a good rhythm so that the pony steps cleanly over every pole in the middle of each stride, without clipping or knocking any!

Aim to stay in the centre all the way down the line.

have you got rhythm?

Try the rhythm tester to find out! Use five poles, placed $3\frac{1}{2}$ ft-$4\frac{1}{2}$ ft (1-1.3m) apart. Now take away pole four, so there is a bigger gap between the last two. Trot through and see if you reach the end correctly, even with one missing. Counting out the strides will help.

variations

More experienced ponies and riders might like to try:
● Setting a line of poles across the diagonal of the school. You will need to work at keeping energy up round the corner with lots of inside leg, and making a flowing line round the turns.
● Setting poles in a circle. This is a bit more tricky, as you and your pony both have to work harder to stay balanced and central.
● Raising poles slightly off the ground, making the pony pick his feet up higher.
● Cantering down a line of poles (set at the 8-9ft distance). Do a few large circles first. You may need to sit down into the saddle to help your pony stay balanced and stop him rushing on down a line of canter poles.

Relax!
Pole-work is brilliant for settling down fizzy ponies. If your pony rushes his jumps, or gets excited even at the sight of them, find out more in our troubleshooting section on pages 54-61.

More experienced partnerships can try a line of poles set at the correct distance for cantering. Stop your pony from picking up too much speed and help him to stay balanced by sitting down more.

Ponies' strides vary in length. The poles will be the correct distance apart for your pony when his footfalls come exactly in between them.

tip for the top
If you are using a line of poles at trot distance (4-4$\frac{1}{2}$ ft / 1.2-1.3m apart), set out an odd number, such as three, five or seven. An even number can confuse the pony who may try hopping over two at a time.

getting going with grids

No problem with poles? Then moving on to try a 'real' jump will be easy. Our next step is to add a small fence, such as a cross-pole of about 12-15ins (38cm) high, 7-8ft (2.1-2.4m) beyond the line of poles on the ground. Pole-work has given you an idea of what it feels like when your pony picks his feet up higher and stretches his neck down to avoid stumbling over them. Now we are going to make him bounce up that bit higher. Let's see if you can keep your good position and stay with his movement down this simple 'grid'.

A grid is any combination of poles on the ground and low jumps set out in a line. Whether you are a nervous novice or already a champion, nothing is better at perfecting your jump sense than working at grids.

Riding your first jump

Don't suddenly panic just because there is a small fence ahead! The poles will already have got you going in a steady trot and placed you in exactly the right spot, so popping over the fence at the end will be simple.

The pony will hardly need to make any extra effort over this low fence. All you need to do is:
● Approach from a wide arc, aiming for the centre of the line of poles.
● Come in at an active and bouncy trot.
● Keep straight.
● Stay balanced.
● Keep using your legs to encourage the pony on.
● Look up beyond the fence.
● Allow your hands to go with the pony and try to absorb the movement of his jump into your legs and hips (you won't need to get into proper jumping position over this height of fence).

Come in at a nice brisk trot, looking up and in the direction you intend to go.

First time around, your pony may hesitate slightly and stretch his head down to look at the new obstacle. Keep looking up and urge him on with your legs.

When he lands, the pony will probably go on in canter. Don't try to pull him back to trot straight away. Get used to recovering your balance and a good canter position as soon as possible after a fence. Let your pony do a few nice, steady canter strides before bringing him back to trot. After all, once you go on to jumping a course you will want to be cantering towards the next fence.

What's so great about grids?

Grid-work (sometimes called 'gymnastic jumping') is brilliant for ponies and for riders. It:

● Boosts confidence.
● Gives a sense of rhythm.
● Improves co-ordination and balance.
● Increases suppleness and agility.
● Teaches quick reactions.
● Allows you to progress as you feel ready.
● And, most of all, it is loads of fun!

The best thing about a well-laid-out grid is that it places the pony on exactly the right stride all the way along the line, so it is easy for him to keep going onwards and easy for you to stay balanced with him. As long as you approach the start straight and with enough energy, stay balanced and keep your legs on, then there is no reason why anything should go wrong. Relax, go with him, and enjoy it!

A second small fence set up one canter stride beyond the first will really get you into the swing.

Time for two

You will be surprised how quickly you are whizzing down that grid as if you have been doing it all your life! Once you are happy and confident, the instructor will change the arrangement slightly. She may well add a second fence about 16-18ft (4.8-5.4m) further on, perhaps with another pole on the ground midway between the two fences.

This straightforward grid will allow you to trot in, pop over the first fence, take one stride of canter over the middle pole, then be perfectly placed to jump out over the second fence.

Try a new challenge by taking away some of the poles in front of the first fence. Leave just one, about 8ft (2.4m) away, helping you arrive at a good point for take-off.

Bouncing along

When a pony lands over one fence and then takes off again immediately in his next stride, without taking a non-jumping stride first, this is called a 'bounce'. Using an occasional bounce fence within a grid really helps strengthen your seat, improve your suppleness and test your reactions!

Fences set at 'bounce' distances make the pony land and then take off again in the very next stride. This is a great exercise for sharpening up the reactions and agility of both of you!

types of fence

uprights

A cross-pole is an ideal starter fence, as its shape guides the pony into the centre. As it has no depth and uses one pair of jump stands only, it is described as an **upright** fence. Another common type of upright has a straight pole across the top, with other poles or wooden 'fillers' placed underneath to fill in the gap and make the fence easier for the pony to see.

spreads

When you are jumping uprights happily in your grids, why not try a **spread** fence? A spread has depth, so two sets of jump stands are used to build it. It encourages the pony to round his back and make a good outline over the fence. The pony has to make a bit more effort to jump a spread fence, as he needs to stretch out and use himself more.

A spread may be built up in many different ways. Examples suitable for novice ponies and riders are:

● Two identical cross-poles, one behind the other
● A cross-pole at the front with a single horizontal pole at the back
● Several poles, or one pole with a filler underneath, at the front, plus a single pole slightly higher at the back.

As you progress, your grids can include both spreads and uprights.

Stay straight, look up, leg on, and you'll sail through that grid.

the grids go up!

Within grids, poles and low fences can be arranged in an endless variety of combinations to improve technique and confidence in ponies and riders. On this page you can learn more about using grids and get some more ideas of grids you can build at home to practise with your own pony. By increasing the difficulty gradually, as you feel ready, you will progress in leaps and bounds!

Grid rules

Follow these ground rules when you are working with grids:

riding the grid

● Approach steadily and straight. Get organised by circling first. At first, stick to riding in a bouncy, active trot.
● Don't rush – you don't need speed, you need balance and bounce.
● Down the grid, focus on trying not to interfere with your pony. Simply close your legs on, look up and keep a steady rein contact. Let your pony canter on once he has entered the grid.
● If there is space, practise approaching from both directions (though make sure the layout is suitable to be jumped from either way).
● Don't do too much in one session. Grids are tiring for your pony.

building the grid

● Start small and simple. Begin with poles on the ground and build up slowly. Only make each exercise more difficult once you and your pony have mastered what you have already put up.
● If you hit problems, lower or simplify things until you are coping confidently again.
● Keep at least the first obstacle

Setting up the grid at the correct distances for your pony is crucial. If it's set out right, he will be perfectly placed for every take-off. Wrong distances will get you both in a mess and soon knock your confidence.

Grids can be used in many different ways to help with problems. This line of bounce cross-poles is useful for slowing a speedy pony. Whatever grid you build, keep the fences small and lower them right down if you have any hiccups.

(called 'element') of your grid as an inviting cross-pole or small upright. Put up the following elements only little by little.

● Give each element a groundline (see right).

● Always use the correct distances for your pony (see below).

● Later you can try approaching in canter. Check you have the correct leading leg on the approach. Remember to open out the distance between the elements of a grid a little following a jump from canter, as the pony will land slightly further out than when he jumps it in trot.

● Remember bounces are tricky and demanding. Increase the number of bounces used as you both get more confident, up to five in a row, but keep the jumps low – use cross-poles and uprights only.

● Spreads in a grid are more difficult than uprights. Until you have more experience, only include a spread at the end of the line.

what is a groundline?

At take-off, a pony loses sight of the fence he is jumping. The only way he gets the size of his leap about right is by memorising the height and width of the jump, and his distance away from it, as he approaches. If there is no pole or filler touching the ground at the front of the jump, this becomes extremely difficult for your pony to do. This is why a single pole with a big gap underneath is one of the hardest fences to jump well. Be fair to your pony and always use a groundline under every fence.

from	pony		horse	
	trot	canter	trot	canter
non-jumping strides 2	30 ft (9m)	31-34ft (9.3-10.2m)	30-32ft (9-9.6m)	34-36ft (10.2-10.8m)
1	16-18ft (4.8-5.4m)	21-24ft (6.3-7.2m)	18ft (5.4m)	24-26ft (7.2-8m)
none (ie, bounce)	9-10ft (2.7-3m)	10-12ft (3-3.6m)	9-11ft (2.7-3.3m)	11-14ft (3.3-4.2m)

Distances

No two ponies have exactly the same stride length, but try the averages above and adjust your distances accordingly. Measure one of your own paces and you will soon learn to walk out the right distances without needing a tape measure. As a rough guide, a child's pace is usually about 2 ft (60cm) long and an adult's about 3 ft (just under 1m). When pacing out a distance between fences, allow about 6 ft (1.8m) afterwards for landing and in front of the next one for taking off.

Two cross-poles one behind the other like the one shown top (called 'parallel' cross-poles), make an inviting small spread. A bigger spread like the one above should only be used for experienced ponies. Notice how both fences have groundlines.

some ideas for DIY grids

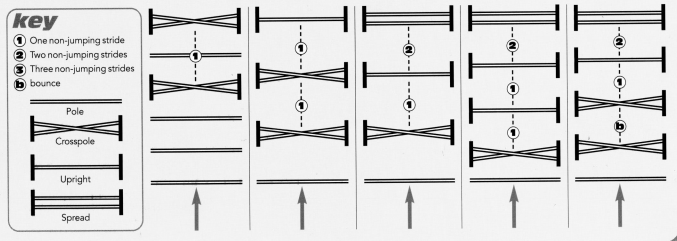

key

① One non-jumping stride
② Two non-jumping strides
③ Three non-jumping strides
ⓑ bounce

Pole

Crosspole

Upright

Spread

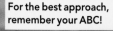
For the best approach, remember your ABC!

facing fences – the right approach

Once you are winging down that grid without a worry, keeping in balance and rhythm all the way, it's time to try some single fences.

There is one thing you are sure to have noticed by now. When you managed to come in exactly right, you popped along the line with no problem. But if your approach happened to go wrong, somehow everything went from bad to worse!

Getting the approach right every time is *the* big secret of jumping.

A good approach sets the pony up to take off well and gives him the best chance to clear the jump. It makes jumping easy.

Grids are great because, with the fences set out at perfect distances, the pony cannot help but reach each one exactly in the right spot to take off. As a result, he keeps up a lovely rhythm, which helps you swing along with no problems.

But coming in to a single fence on its own, *you* have to find that rhythm and balance, and keep it! Sloppy approaches won't do. Each approach must be planned with precision. Instead of just focusing on your position and being carried into the fences by your pony, now you are going to have to really *ride* him into them.

the right recipe

How can you make sure your pony arrives at the fence with all four legs organised and without getting himself in a mess? Every good approach has the same ingredients. It must be:

Active
Balanced
Central

A, B, C – that's easy to remember! We will look at these one at a time, seeing how things go wrong and how to get them going right.

A get active!

Even if a fence is small, you will only get over it if your pony has enough 'oomph'. This is important right from the start, but it becomes crucial as the fences get bigger. The mistake many riders make, however, is to confuse 'oomph' with speed.

Picture the top show jumpers. Even in a jump-off, they are rarely seen to gallop at a fence. The impression is one of *power* and *control*. You may only be aiming to go clear over a 2-ft fence, but the idea is exactly the same. We are looking not for speed but for POWER, contained where it is needed, in the pony's engine – his hindquarters. In horse-speak, this contained power is called 'impulsion'. Impulsion creates bounce, and it is *bounce* that gets the pony into the air and clear over the fence.

Wow – look at all that pent-up power...

how can I get impulsion?

Create impulsion by revving up the pony's engine (his back end), but keeping the brake on. Then he steps further underneath his body, like this.

Compare the flat, strung-out canter above with the bouncy, collected one below.

Impulsion is created when the pony is trying to take faster or bigger steps with his hindlegs, bringing them further underneath his body, but is being held back from simply running on faster by the rider's rein aids. He becomes like a coiled-up spring – he wants to go forward more, but he can't until the rider releases the spring.

When a pony tanks at top speed towards a fence, stretched out like a beanpole, this is what happens:

● The pony is in control. He can run out or stop whenever he feels like it.

● All his weight is on his front end. It will be difficult to get into the air.

● His 'outline' is flat and hollow. He will not be able to make the rounded bascule needed to clear a jump with any height.

● He will not have enough time to judge the size of the jump or his take-off point accurately. He may find he takes off too far away, or has to put in an extra stride at the last minute, bringing him too close to pick his front legs up in time.

When a pony is brought into the fence with an active but bouncy stride, he really lifts and 'rounds' over it. Even if this had been a big fence, this pony would have cleared it with no problem.

In the picture above the pony is approaching in balance, with a good rhythm (we'll talk about these next). The rider is using her legs to create real impulsion from her pony's hindquarters. But she isn't letting all that energy whoosh out the front end and disappear. She is holding it in with a steady, even contact on the reins.

This rider has her pony 'between hand and leg' (a term you may hear your riding instructor use). Her pony is going to find it easy to take off and clear a fence, whatever its height.

● The rider is the driver, not just a passenger.

● She is creating energy in the pony's 'engine' (his hindquarters), so he can push off over any size of fence.

● She is containing that energy with her hands, so creating bounce!

● The rounded outline this creates will make it easy for the pony to take off cleanly and bascule over the fence.

● The steady approach gives plenty of time to assess the jump and take-off.

try this

half-halt

Half-halt is a brilliant trick to steady a pony and create more bounce at the same time, all in just one or two strides. Get the hang of it and your flat-work and jumping will both improve no end. Top riders in the dressage and jumping arenas are constantly using half-halts to re-balance their horses and set them up for a change of pace, direction or approach to a fence. But they do it so well you would hardly notice! Half-halt also reminds the horse to pay attention, preparing him for a new instruction such as a turn or transition.

A half-halt is a momentary check by the rider. It uses the same aids as for halt, but, instead of allowing the pony to come to a stop, it just steadies him briefly and asks him to round his back and bring his hindquarters further underneath his body.

● Close your legs against the pony's sides to send him forwards. Sit deep in the saddle. The instant you feel him moving on more actively, instead of following the movement with your hands, squeeze on the reins (don't move your hands backwards though) and brace your back slightly.

● Practise in walk first. This is an exercise you can try out hacking as well as in the school.

● If your pony jolts to a halt, you have been too strong with your hands and kept the pressure up too long. If he pulls and leans on the bit, you have used too much leg.

facing fences – a balancing act

With four legs and a heavy head and body to sort out, a pony needs to get himself super-organised to jump a fence. Add a wobbly, wriggling rider on his back and you can see how it's not such a straightforward job as many ponies make it look. And so we come to the B of our A-B-C of the perfect approach – BALANCE.

B get balanced!

Would you fancy doing a hurdles race, or a high jump, carrying a hefty rucksack – or a squirming chimpanzee – on your back? Now imagine trying it with two extra legs! Your pony needs you to stay as still as possible in the saddle and not interfere.

Heading for those hurdles, or that high jump, how would you approach? Long, flat strides may get there quickly, but you would then find it difficult to get into the air. Short, cramped strides would make it very hard to keep up enough forward movement. For the best take-off, you would use even, medium-length strides, trying to stay as balanced as possible.

A pony is exactly the same, only getting his body set up for a good jump is slightly more complicated, due to having an extra two legs – and a rider on his back! Too long a stride makes a pony jump flat. Too slow, or restricted a stride means he cramps up and 'bucks' over the fence instead of flowing over it. Both wrong approaches are likely to be unsteady and unbalanced, risking a refusal, bad take-off or knockdown.

How can I balance my pony better?

A good rider will think about using her seat and other aids to help her pony get 'together' and organised as he approaches a fence.

● When schooling, set yourselves up in good balance by circling before approaching a fence.
● Remember that a pony will never be balanced in canter if he is on the wrong leading leg. Always get on to

Poles on the ground are great for improving bounce, balance and beat!

the correct (inside) lead before you head for a fence in canter.
● Aim for a steady but bouncy pace, with a regular rhythm to the stride. Use your inside leg to make the pony step underneath his body with his hindlegs (see the previous page). Keep an even, equal contact on both reins.
● The position of the head makes a lot of difference to the pony's balance. Use your legs and an even, steady contact to keep his head up enough to see the fence, but not flung high trying to escape your control.
● On the turn towards the fence, use plenty of inside leg to keep your pony upright and stop him veering in, motorbike-style. Try not to tip your body to one side.

tip for the top

Look back a page to see how half-halts can help re-balance your pony quickly if he is running on too fast or has too much weight on his front end.

Your pony won't be balanced if you are all over the place on his back. Try to sit, and give your aids, as quietly as you can.

A pony with his head stuck up in the air will be hollow and stiff through his back and take uneven, awkward strides.

Rhythm counts

Rhythm goes hand in hand with balance. It is important, because it helps everything to FLOW. A pony taking even, rhythmical strides will be well balanced and both of you will be able to judge his take-off more easily. You will be ready for whatever obstacle comes along.

To get the bouncy canter you want, work at getting your pony to accept your rein contact, 'round' through his back and make even, rhythmical strides.

try this

in the beat

Work at getting a good rhythm by thinking of a favourite song that has got an even, regular beat to it. Sing it out loud as you canter along and turn towards a fence! Too embarrassing? Then count out the strides, trying to make each one come at the same tempo right up to and over the fence. Or say "Can-ter, can-ter, can-ter" in time with the stride. Try this at every approach and you will soon find yourself relaxing into a tempo – and taking off at the same time as your pony without even thinking about it!

Aiming for the centre of the fence will help you stay balanced.

plan ahead for accuracy

Over-shooting the turn or drifting to one side is asking for a run-out.

C get central!

The final part of the A-B-C is C for CENTRAL – in other words, take it straight!

Taking fences on angles is best left to jump-off experts. For now, always aim for the middle of every jump, because this gives the pony the best chance of judging the fence accurately and taking off in balance. It also discourages any ideas he might have about running out to one side. And in many styles of fence, such as cross-poles and some other designs, the central part is also intended to be the easiest and most inviting place to jump, so it makes sense to aim for it.

● Come round towards each fence in a wide, even semicircle. Then you can use the turn to help get your pony balanced.
● Look towards the fence so that your head, shoulders and upper body are already making the turn and directing the pony around it.
● Plan ahead and judge the turn, so that as you come around to face the fence you can head directly for it. Don't cut in too sharply, or overshoot and have to haul your pony back on line.

try this

going straight

Use a marker, such as a cone, to guide you around the perfect turn into the fence (you can set one up for each fence in a course). Later, try riding the same approaches without the marker and see if you can get the same accuracy and an even turn.

There are some suggestions to help with ponies who drift to one side on page 59.

Use a marker such as a barrel or cone to practise making a balanced, even turn that will bring you straight to the centre of the fence.

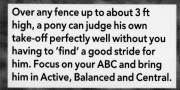

Over any fence up to about 3 ft high, a pony can judge his own take-off perfectly well without you having to 'find' a good stride for him. Focus on your ABC and bring him in Active, Balanced and Central.

facing fences –
wait for it!

If you are coming up to a fence with bounce and in balance, then the jump itself should be no problem, as long as you remember one more golden rule – wait for the fence to come to you!

Lots of riders get themselves in quite a stew on the approach to a fence. They're not really concentrating on their ABC. They're frantically thinking to themselves, "Where's the take-off point? Where's that take-off point? Help!"

Once this worry about 'seeing a stride' gets a hold, the temptation to hurry the pony towards the fence, anxiously trying to hold him back or urge him on to reach what you think is a good take-off point, is very strong. It becomes all too easy to lose your position and worry or confuse your pony so that he jumps badly – or not at all.

Take your time

Think positive. Instead of having the thought "Where is it?", focus on the thought, "Just wait, we're coming" (perhaps you can even whisper this to yourself, in time with the pony's movement). As long as you keep moving forwards with that regular, rhythmic and bouncy stride, you will arrive relaxed, in

good time, and your pony will be able to jump well, however high the fence.

'Looking for a stride' is a skill to be learned when you get into jumping seriously. The trouble with learner-jumpers trying to judge the take-off point for themselves is that it only creates a tense, worried approach where the rider is interfering too much. Then what tends to happen is that when you think you have 'seen' the stride, you drop the reins and kick. This leaves the poor pony in the lurch, with all his weight on his front end, at the very moment he needs to be held together with all his impulsion in his hindquarters.

Often he ends up jumping long and flat and knocks the fence down. Or he may put in an extra, awkward last-minute stride, or stop altogether.

● Use your legs to keep your pony going forwards and balanced.
● Keep contact with the reins to stop him speeding up too much and to help him stay balanced.

Leave 'looking for a stride' to the experts!

Interfere too much and tell your pony when to "go", and the chances are you'll get it wrong.

Learn to hold that energy in, and wait for the fence to come to you.

positive *thinking*

When you start jumping single fences, you must mean business. Be determined. Horses and ponies seem to have a sixth sense that tells them if their rider isn't really committed. Somehow, the message seems to go straight down the reins. A pony can quickly lose confidence and start stopping if you don't ride positively. Be convinced yourself, and you will convince your pony!

If you want your pony to put the effort in, you'll have to do the same. Tackling single fences needs positive riding.

try this

using placing poles

To help you progress from grids to single fences, it is a good idea to use placing poles – a pole placed on the ground a little way in front of the fence to help the pony arrive at the right take-off point.

● Start by approaching in trot. For this, the pole should be about 8ft (2.4m) in front of the fence. Let your pony canter on afterwards, but bring him back to trot to approach next time.

● When this is going well, try approaching in canter. For canter, the pole should be 16-18ft (4.8-5.4m) away to allow the pony to take one stride between it and the fence. Try setting up two or three fences with placing poles at different positions around the arena.

● Once you are both happy with this exercise, try moving the placing pole back to about 30ft (9m) before the fence. This gives two strides in between the pole and the fence. Now move the pole to about 45ft (13.5m). Can you fit exactly three strides in? If so, you're getting good! You are ready to practise approaching without the help of a placing pole at all.

Using placing poles in front of the fence gives both the pony and rider confidence that the take off will be right.

facing fences –
happy landings

By now it is obvious that the route to a clear round involves plenty more than simply pointing your pony at a jump and hoping for the best. The way the jump is approached has a great deal to do with getting to the other side in good style.

But, of course, getting over one fence neatly is not the end of the story! To make the jump-off, the pony and rider team have to learn to tackle every fence without a mistake. So every approach must be right.

When you ride one fence at a time, there is plenty of time to perfect your approach and to recover and reorganise yourself afterwards. No excuses for not getting things right! This goes for the first fence in a course, too.

But when it comes to going on to another fence, then another and another, how you arrive at each one depends on how much in control you were landing over the one before. Finish up in a heap after fence one, and the chances are you are not going to be organised in time to give fence two your best shot.

So, although, at first, landing stylishly may not seem too important (you are probably just relieved to get over at all!), it is well worth getting it right from the start, as it will become more and more important once you progress to tackling fences grouped together.

Let's take a closer look at what happens over the jump. How can you land on the other side looking ready for the next challenge?

Even landing over a low fence, the joints of the pony's forelegs have to absorb a lot of shock. You can lessen the jarring by staying in balance up on top.

tip
for the
top

Keep fences small, even as you both progress. The idea is to improve your skills and technique, not to see how high your pony can jump. If you want to be more ambitious, widen spread fences a little, which will teach your pony to 'round' more. Even an experienced pair need not practise over fences of more than 2ft 6ins to 3ft.

As the pony comes down, bring your body more upright again, keeping your lower leg underneath you and head up. Now you are in a good position to stay in balance as you canter on.

Having his rider tipping forwards on to his neck has forced all this pony's weight on to his front end. She is very insecure and is going to struggle to get him balanced and bouncing again ready for the next fence.

Over and down

Keeping a good position in the saddle over the fence and during the landing helps the pony remain balanced all the way. Then he can carry on to the next fence with the minimum of readjustment. It also lessens the amount of jarring on his legs, which take quite a pounding as he comes down.

● As the pony lands, he raises his head. Keep a light contact on the reins. Avoid hanging on to his mouth to steady yourself.

● Move your legs forward a little for security, but try to stay in your 'squashed down' position over small fences. If you sit up too early, the weight on your pony's quarters could make him bring his back legs down too quickly and knock the fence.

● Stay looking up towards the next obstacle.

● As the hindlegs come down, sit gently into the saddle without bumping. Straighten your back and take care not to tip to one side.

Aim to get organised and ready for action again within the next stride or two – the sign of a good rider!

Left: By all means look towards the next fence as you land, ready to plan the next approach. But always ride a few strides in a straight line, so your pony does not get into the habit of veering to one side after a fence.

Right: Practise a tidy get-away after every fence you jump, even if there are no more to follow. Then neither of you will get into the habit of sloppy landings!

homework on the flat

Set yourself up for a useful jumping session by limbering up on the flat first, getting your pony to pay attention to your aids.

Impulsion, balance, rhythm, straightness – so these aren't just for dressage riders! The better a pony works on the flat, the better he will jump.

Here are some flat-work exercises that will not only help to make your pony a more supple and obedient ride, but directly improve his jumping too, by helping him to listen to your signals and get that rhythm between the jumps and a correct approach every time.

try this

bend it!

Why? Every jumping course includes turns and changes of direction. You need to make accurate turns and keep your pony balanced through every one without losing impulsion. He can only do this if he is supple, not stiff.

Exercises to help: Large (20-metre) circles. Turns across the school. Figures of eight. Serpentines. Shoulder-in.

Practice points:

● Use all circles and turns (even just going around the corners of the school) to insist your pony bends through his whole body. He should be flexing towards the inside of the bend or circle.

● Use your inside leg on the girth to stop the pony 'falling in' to the turn. Your outside leg just behind the girth will stop the quarters swinging out. Avoid simply pulling his neck in, leaving the quarters sticking out.

● Ask the pony to look slightly to the inside with little upward (not backward) squeezes on the inside rein. You want to just be able to see his inside eye. Don't create a dead pull, as this will only make him stiffen. Allow your outside hand forward just a little as you ask, so he can flex his neck, but try to keep an even, steady weight in both reins.

● Look up, between the pony's ears. Keep your shoulders in line with his – don't lean in or swing one shoulder back.

● Try to keep up the energy of the strides, even around the corner. Give a little nudge with your inside heel with each stride.

● Only progress to smaller (15-metre) circles once you have a bouncy, balanced stride in larger ones.

Lots of inside leg will help keep him balanced through the turn.

did you know?

Top horses are hardly ever jumped at home between shows. Riders concentrate on improving obedience and suppleness with work on the flat.

● Work in walk, then trot. When you have achieved turns and circles in a balanced, active trot, try canter, checking you are using the correct (inside) leading leg.

● Move on to exercises like trotting figures of eight and serpentines, to get him used to changing the bend in his body alternately from one side to the other.

Your pony will never be able to make a balanced turn if he is stiff and looking to the outside. Use all sorts of corners, turns and circles to make him more supple.

Riding straight is not as easy as it seems!

try this

going straight

Why? So the pony becomes equally supple on both sides of his body. He will then be easy to turn and to steer towards the centre of a fence.

Exercises to help: Straight lines down and across the school in walk and trot.

Practice points:
● Sit up tall. Look ahead and keep your shoulders level.
● Try to keep an even weight in both hands and onto both seat-bones.
● Keep your legs on. It is much easier to keep straight when the pony is going forwards actively than when he is dawdling along.

tip for the top

Shoulder-in really helps a pony learn to bend around a turn. Bring the front end slightly in off the track, as if you were going to ride a circle. Then use lots of inside leg to make the pony bend to the inside but actually keep going ahead. Little squeezes on the inside rein ask him to look that way. The outside hand and leg control the amount of bend.

try this

instant impulsion

Why? Clever jumping ponies need to give you that springy, rounded canter, on the correct leading leg, straight away whenever you ask for it. They must be able to keep it up right up to and over the fence. This means being very attentive and also supple all the way through the body, from the front to the back, as well as on both sides.

Exercises to help:
Transitions. Half-halts.

Practice points:
● Work on immediate, obedient transitions. Aim to get your pony going forwards to trot from a slight nudge of the heels. If he is lazy and takes no notice, flick him quickly behind the girth with your schooling whip. He will soon get the idea. Practise until he reacts instantly, then try trot to canter. When you are getting really good at it, try walk to canter transitions.
● Don't surprise your pony by suddenly booting him in the ribs, expecting him to instantly react. Make sure you already have his attention with a good rein contact and positive seat. If he is listening to you, waiting for the next signal, he is much more likely to react quickly, as long as the aids you give are clear. Preparation is particularly important for 'indirect' transitions, eg halt>trot, or walk>canter.
● Don't neglect your downward transitions. They should be smooth and balanced too. Try not to think of pulling back to slow down or the transition will be jerky and you will lose all your steadiness and momentum. Concentrate on riding forwards, keeping your legs on so the hindlegs keep stepping underneath. Now sit down into the saddle, imagining you are pushing your hips and chest forward towards the pony's neck. Stop following his head movement with your hands, making them resist slightly, and he will slow.
● Give yourself lots of transition practice by doing just a few strides of each pace – walk to trot to walk again, or trot to canter to trot. Or use the school markers to make your changes of pace. Be strict with yourself!

tip for the top

Like us, ponies are left or right-sided. Do plenty of work in the direction of your pony's stiffer side to help supple it. Don't neglect his 'good' side though. Start off in that direction to warm him up.

Asking for canter on a bend will help your pony strike off on to the correct leg. Aim for instant transitions up and down and to stay in balance all the time.

clever combinations

Over the last pages you have learned how to ride up to, over and away from a single fence. Now it is time to start putting those lessons into practice by linking fences together. Anyone who has done a bit of jumping will tell you that it is one thing being able to keep your position and control over a single obstacle. But tackle more than one fence at a time and things can easily go wrong – if you are not prepared!

What is a combination?

A series of fences built closely together is called a combination. It has a set distance between each 'element' of either one or two canter strides. Two elements make up a 'double' and three a 'treble'.

A show jumping course is made up from a mixture of single fences and combinations. In top competition, the course builder will ask the horses and riders many difficult questions by mixing different types of fences within a combination, or setting slightly tricky distances between the elements. For novices, however, combination distances should be straightforward, so the pony flows on from one jump to the next – as long as he gets the approach to the first one right!

Distance data

Distances between the fences in a combination are the same as those given on page 23 for grid exercises,

To pace out distances, stand with your back against the landing side of the first element. Take even paces towards the next. In combinations set at 'true' distances for the average pony's stride, allow two paces for landing, four for each non-jumping stride, and two for the next take-off.

A double is made up from two elements marked A and B. In this picture the double consists of a spread in, with one non-jumping stride to an upright out.

except that the course builder always assumes the approach will be in canter.

When you are building combinations to practise over at home, do remember, however, that if your first element is a spread, the pony will land slightly further out over it. To allow for this and avoid the central distance then becoming too short for comfort, add an extra 6ins (15cm) per stride.

combination checklist

● When practising at home, work out the distances between the elements carefully so they are correct for your pony, or he may find it difficult or impossible to take off at the second/third element.
● Start practising using two strides in between two fences. Later, add a third fence to make a 'treble'. One-strided, or bounce combinations, are harder, so leave these until you are going on confidently.
● For novice riders or ponies, only use a spread fence as the first element. A spread in the middle or going out of a combination is more demanding.
● Use ascending spreads and small parallels and uprights (see p.40/41) only.

Keep looking up and riding on strongly all the way, or your pony may run out of steam in the middle!

● Remember to ride straight for the centre of all the elements.
● Look up as you approach, and all the way through.
● Keep using your legs between the fences, to keep up that forward momentum.
● Keep a light contact on the reins. Don't 'drop' your pony in the middle!

Straightness is crucial. If you start drifting, a run-out is guaranteed.

A treble is made up from three elements, marked A, B and C. This one involves a spread followed by two strides to an upright, the[n] [one] stride to another upright.

try this

lengthening and shortening

Why? To jump through a combination clear, you may have to ask the pony to take longer, or shorter, strides to arrive at the right place to take off. With more experience, you will be able to lengthen and shorten strides to arrive at single fences more accurately too, or to save time in a jump off.

Exercises to try: Lengthening and shortening the stride on the flat.

Practice points:

● Lengthening the stride is not the same as going faster, and shortening does not mean going slower. The aim is to keep the same speed, balance and bounce, but either to take fewer, longer steps or more, shorter ones.

● Get a good active trot with lots of impulsion, not speed (use your half-halts). To ask for lengthening, really push with your legs and seat as you do the 'sit' beat of the trot. Allow just a little with your hands. Ask for a few strides, then come back to normal 'working' trot.

● Shorten the stride by using half-halts to make your pony more gathered up or 'collected'. But keep up the oomph!

● Lengthening, in particular, takes lots of practice, so keep trying to get it right, remembering you want more power, not speed. Try in canter once you have got the idea in trot.

● Use the different sides of the school to practise. Ask for lengthening down the long side, or across the diagonal, then shortening across the short side.

The long and the short of it

Different ponies have different lengths of stride. But an instructor in a group lesson, or a course builder at a novice show, has to set the distances in a combination at an average that he hopes will suit most of the ponies.

Practise assessing how the pony you are riding goes. Does he have a particularly short stride? Then you know you will have to push him on that little bit more when approaching the combination and between the elements. Then we will take larger steps and will reach the second (and third) fences without having to put in an extra, awkward, stride.

If your pony takes particularly long strides, come in on a compact, bouncy canter. Sit up and try to collect him between the elements. If you let him run on, you will be arriving at the next part before he has fitted in the right number of strides comfortably.

try this

Can you make it?

Here is an exercise to help you and your pony get used to adjusting your strides within a combination. Put a take-off pole about 2ft (60cm) in front of a small upright and another pole two strides (31-34ft/9.3-10.2m) behind. Canter in and, on landing, count the two strides to the pole. Now roll the pole out about 3ft (90cm) further and again ride two strides to it – you will have to lengthen to reach it this time! You can also try shortening the distance (to around 29-30ft (8.7-9m), but go back to the medium distance first.

Practise lengthening and shortening the canter stride, so your pony can cope if he needs to stretch out or gather himself up to arrive correctly at the second or third elements of a combination.

riding a course

tip for the top

First fences can even catch out the best! Get your pony's attention before turning in to the first fence, so he knows the action is about to begin. Ride forward with positive aids.

Once you are taking on single fences and combinations there's no reason why you shouldn't fly around a simple course. Most novice courses consist of between eight and 10 fences and include at least one combination. Don't be daunted at the thought of facing this number of jumps one after another. Just remember the all-important skills you have learned so far.

course catchwords

on the approach
● Get a rhythmic, bouncy but not-too-fast canter. Ride positively into each fence.
● Look towards your fence and come round to it in a wide arc, so there is plenty of time and space to get it right. Head straight for the centre.
● Have your legs on your pony's sides to keep that impulsion up, ready to give extra encouragement if needed.
● Keep your bottom just out of the saddle, unless you need to steady him back or push him on more, in which case sit deep and tall.
● Keep a firm and steady but 'elastic' contact on the reins. Don't interfere, but don't leave your pony to his own devices either.
● Let the fence come to you. Just focus on your position and think rhythm ("can-ter, can-ter, can-ter").

in the air
● Keep that good jump position – legs underneath you, chest squashed down, hands 'giving'. Look ahead where you are going, not down – if you have hit the fence, it's too late!

getting away
● Look at and think about the next obstacle straight away. Sit tall and re-balance your pony as quickly as you can. Remember – only you know the course!

Don't look down – it's too late!

Use all the space you have to make wide, steady turns, and reorganise yourself between the fences. Use a cone to mark a good place for each turn in practice.

Right-on rhythm

Though the fences are tackled one at a time, to add up to a clear round you need to aim for a flowing performance the whole way around. At first, you may decide there is a fence or two you would prefer to take from trot to get more control. But if your pony lands in canter, try not to keep pulling him back to trot or he will get confused and out of balance. Work towards keeping up a lovely rhythmic canter from start to finish.

Walk talk

If you watch superstar show jumpers or event riders in action, they literally seem to *flow* from one fence to the next. This is not only because they have great technique (all the things we have learned about so far). They are also ultra-organised about how they are going to jump the course before they even enter the arena.

When it comes to jumping a course in a competition, whatever the height or difficulty of the jumps, every rider needs to prepare thoroughly for every round they do by walking around the route they plan to take on foot first. 'Walking the course' is your chance to get the course as a whole firmly in your head and to plan how you are going to ride it.

As you walk around, concentrate on:

The order Are you sure you know which order to jump the fences in? You will be eliminated (disqualified) for going wrong. The jumps will be clearly numbered, but shut your eyes and ride the course in your mind to make sure it has stuck!

The route The route you take between each fence is called your 'track'. Walk the exact line you plan to ride. That means going deep into each corner and using the whole arena or field to get a good approach to every fence. Leave short-cuts for when you reach the timed jump-off.

The pace How much impulsion is each fence going to need? Remember, spread fences will need a little more 'oomph'.

The distances Combinations will need spot-on riding. Don't just aim and hope for the best. Pace out the distance between the elements so you know exactly how many strides to take to flow through the combination easily.

Warning! Avoid possible stops by forward planning. Look out for especially spooky patterned or shaped fences, jumps heading away from the collecting ring (or, at home, the field gate), or placed next to the spectator ropes. Ride extra-strongly at these. Be prepared!

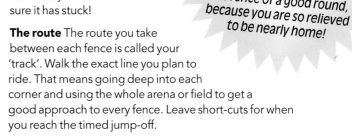

Concentration is the name of the game. Keep thinking all the way round the course. It is easy to fluff the last fence of a good round, because you are so relieved to be nearly home!

Above: Look out for spooky or awkwardly-placed fences that could make your pony think twice.

Left: Walking the course carefully beforehand is essential preparation for that clear round in showjumping or cross-country events.

practice makes *perfect*

Course-riding skills can be polished up with the help of the exercises on this page. Before you start each schooling session, however, don't forget these homework 'musts':

When jumping at home, keep the fences small and don't lose sight of safety.

● Never jump alone. Life is much easier if someone else is around to move fences and pick up the poles (or you, if you happen to fall off!).
● Use an enclosed area with level, safe ground.
● Loosen up with some flat-work.
● Begin with simple, familiar exercises. Keep fences small.
● Don't overdo it. Jumping is hard work for a pony. Forty minutes is plenty at a time, and two or three times a week is enough. Be sensible in summer when the ground is hard and jarring on a pony's feet.

All change

During a course, it is easy to lose impulsion and balance around the turns and changes of direction, causing your pony to flatten and lose bounce on the approach to the next fence. Badly-ridden corners account for many faults in the ring. So get in as much practice you can at making balanced turns and changes in direction and being able to swap your pony's leading canter leg quickly and efficiently.

Using plenty of inside leg around every turn will help keep your pony active and balanced.

tip for the top

When making a turn, use lots of inside leg. This will keep your pony's inside hindfoot stepping underneath him and helps to keep your pony's head up. Then his whole body will stay balanced instead of leaning into the turn – as long as you keep your outside rein firm and steady too!

Learn to *ask* your pony to land with a particular canter leg leading, rather than leaving it to chance.

Putting two small uprights at a right angle to each other gives you several choices of approach and the opportunity to practise doing wide, balanced turns.

try this

changing canter leads

Lay two poles out parallel to each other with around 8-9ft (2.4-2.7m) in between. Ride down between them in trot. Ask for canter as you go through. Try to get canter before you reach the end of the poles!

Ask for the leading leg on your pony's most supple side first. Head off on that rein and come around again in a large circle. As you approach the poles again, ask for trot. Through the poles, ask for canter again. Do several circles on this rein, coming back to trot each time then asking for canter between the poles. Now change the rein and go the other way.

Once you get good, try alternating the direction you go. Head off on the right-hand lead one time, then aim for left canter the next. It's tricky!

try this

figure of eight

Set up a small cross-pole in the centre of your schooling area. Ride large circles in trot on your pony's most supple side, popping over the fence as you come round to it. You'll notice that the pony will land in canter. Check quickly to see if he is on the correct lead, and if he isn't, bring him back to trot straight away and correct it. Now try the same thing going in the other direction.

There is no need to leave the canter lead your pony lands on to chance. Ask for him to land on the correct leg by using your inside hand to turn his head slightly that way, giving a little nudge with your inside heel and moving your outside leg slightly behind the girth as you go over the fence.

Once you are going well on each rein, try a figure of eight.

As you land over the cross-pole, head off in the other direction, so you are going alternately on each rein. You will need your wits about you to get the correct lead every time!

try this

two together

Set up two small fences at a right angle to each other. Put a placing pole 16-18ft (4.8-5.4m) in front of each. Approach the first fence in trot. Let your pony canter on for a few strides afterwards, then bring him back to trot. Make a wide turn round to approach the other fence and do the same.

As you get more confident, try letting your pony canter on around the turn if he is on the correct leg. If he is wrong, come back to trot and strike off again.

try this

make it four

Set up four small cross-poles in a large square or figure of eight shape. Each one needs a placing pole at about 16-18ft (4.8-5.4m) in front. There should be a measured number of strides between fences one and two and fences three and four.

Approach fence one in trot. Canter on to fence two. Check you have landed on the correct leading leg (if you haven't, trot briefly then strike off again), then make a wide turn around to fences three and four. Keep going around the figure of eight. If things are going well, try it without the placing poles.

Positioning three small fences like this, or using four, to make up the sides of a square, creates lots of options for turning and approaching from different directions.

making the difference

Now that you have learned quite a bit about jumping, you will know that, even though one course of jumps may look like another, nothing could be more wrong!

A jumping class at a show is not simply a business of sticking up a few fences in a field and waiting to see whose horse can jump highest! A skilful course designer can test his competitors by changing the difficulty of a fence in many ways besides making it bigger.

International courses will be packed full of problems for the horse and rider to work out. But even at novice level, a good course will test the training of the pony and the skill of the rider by posing a few challenges. As each course you encounter will be different, the more courses you can tackle, the more experienced you will become about how best to answer those questions.

Uprights take very accurate jumping, particularly as they go up in size.

riding different types of fence

Here is a selection of the types of jump you may find included in a course at a show. You can recreate most of them at home and include them in your practice courses.

uprights are tricky to jump accurately, especially as they increase in size. This is because, to clear an upright, your pony needs to reach the highest point of his leap exactly over the top of the fence. If he takes off too close, he won't get his forelegs up in time. Too far away, and he will probably tip the top pole off behind.

tip ● Make things easier for your pony in practice sessions by putting a pole on the ground just in front of the fence.
● Concentrate on an accurate approach that's balanced and steady.

A stile is an upright designed to be especially narrow. Aim for the centre to avoid a run-out!

narrow fences such as stiles or narrow gates are a test of accuracy, as they are much less inviting than a large, wide fence. Can you aim straight for the centre and avoid a run-out? It is easy for your pony to get distracted, or decide to pass it by instead of making the effort to jump. You must be balanced and active in your approach, but most of all, straight!

tip ● Build a practice fence at home of rails no more than 6ft (1.8m) wide. Look up, focusing on a central spot beyond the fence.
● Use guiding poles placed at an angle to funnel you in, removing them when your pony is jumping confidently.

Planks

Pole & fillers

Wall

related distances

Designers also use 'related distances' in their courses. This involves positioning a jump a set number of average strides after the last one, eg. three, four or five strides.

When you walk the course, pace out any related distances. Aim to get the exact number of strides between the fences that the course builder intended. Remember, if your pony takes particularly long strides, you will need to collect him up to fit these in. If his strides are short, you'll need to ask him to lengthen. You also need to be ready to make adjustments if your pony unexpectedly lands a bit too far out or close to the first of the fences.

● Don't interfere too much between the fences and put the pony off.
● Sit up and use half-halts to steady and re-balance after landing, particularly if you jumped the first fence awkwardly.
● Leg on!

	Ponies	Horses
Three non-jumping strides	44-46ft (13.2-13.8m)	46-48ft (13.8-14.4m)
Four non-jumping strides	55-57ft (16.5-17.1m)	57-60ft (17.1-18m)
Five non-jumping strides	66-68ft (19.8-20.4m)	68-72ft (20.4-21.6m)

An ascending spread is an inviting shape to jump.

ascending spreads
have a front pole lower than the back pole. Again, the pony needs lots of 'go' to clear the full width, but an accurate take-off that doesn't bring him in too close or too far away.

 ● Use lots of leg to create impulsion, but don't increase your speed.

triple bars
are sometimes called 'staircase' fences, because they are three poles deep, with the second and third poles progressively higher. They are inviting to jump, because they are built in the same shape as the arc of the pony's leap. But because the fence is wide, your pony will need plenty of impulsion to make the spread.

 ● Avoid taking off too far away – try to get in as close as you can, but on a bouncy, active stride.

pyramid or hog's back
-shaped spreads are three poles deep, with the highest one in the middle. Again, this is inviting to jump, though it has more width than a simple ascending spread.

 ● This is a useful shape for practising at home, as it can be jumped safely from both directions.

parallels
have the back pole at the same height as the front one. They are the most difficult spreads to jump, as they test the pony's agility and technique – he must jump up as if for an upright, and out, to make the spread. Always approach with as much balance, rhythm and impulsion as you can.

In a parallel, the front and back of the spread are at the same height.

 ● Never build a parallel at home with a 'false' groundline.
● Make things easier for your pony by using a solid filler under the front poles.

ditches and water trays
are sometimes used underneath fences, and always cause drama at shows. Ponies are naturally suspicious of water and holes in the ground, so put in plenty of homework.

 ● Pop over little ditches out on hacks.
● Look over the page to see how to construct a home-made water tray.or ditch.
● A lead from a confident pony will help at first.
● Put a low pole over your ditch or water tray and use angled poles to guide your pony in. Let him look, but insist he goes towards it.

Introduce your pony carefully to water trays and he'll soon be popping over them

combinations
For novice classes, a course designer will usually use a spread as the first fence of a combination, as this encourages the pony to land going forwards, well out so he is placed correctly for the next element.

● An upright into the combination is deceptively tricky, as the pony lands more steeply. So push on as you land to make the distance to the next.
● If you are facing a treble, the same 'rules' apply after the second element, but the danger of losing momentum is even greater – so leg on!
● Practise treble combinations at home using an ascending spread followed by two strides to an upright then two to a small parallel. Keep the fences low. As you get better, reduce the distance between the first two fences to one stride only.

course-building at home

Who says you can't practise at home because you haven't any equipment? Exercises like the ones suggested earlier only require a few poles and stands. With a little imagination, you can practise a whole course too, without the need for dozens of flashy show jumps. As few as three or four fences can create plenty of different courses, especially if you take care to build so each can be jumped from either direction.

Using only a handful of fences means you can make the most of the equipment and the space you have and leave space in the paddock for flat-work too. Become an expert course-builder and you and your pony can have endless fun at home, tuning up your technique all the time.

tip for the top

Don't make the fences too high. Over-facing at home is the quickest way to spoil your pony's fun. It is by practising regularly over small, inviting jumps and improving your skills that you will learn to cope with whatever comes your way in the ring.

course-building tips

Always give your fences a groundline. Although it is not as high, because it does not have a groundline, the fence on the right is harder for a pony to weigh up than the one on the left.

● Include a variety of upright and spread fences.

● Every fence must have a clear groundline on the take-off side, such as a pole on the ground, to help your pony judge its height.

● Only plan to use a fence in both directions if it is designed to be jumped either way. It must have a groundline on both sides.

● A spread with one pole at the back can only be jumped one way. The back pole should never be lower than the front pole. It must not be a plank.

● Begin your course with an inviting fence, such as a cross-pole or small, well-filled-in spread.

● Include a combination in your course if you have enough equipment. Double-check distances between the elements to make sure they are correct.

● Include at least one change of direction, preferably more. Allow plenty of space for turns, so the course can flow and you can get up a nice rhythm with no awkward or sharp corners.

● Make the fences as solid-looking as possible, using as much of your equipment as you can. There are ideas for building your own jumps on pages 44-45.

● Only build practice jumps that will knock down if hit.

● If you are using a pole at an angle, sit it in a cup on the wing stand. Don't balance it on the top pole.

● Allow room for safe approaches on level ground. The minimum area you need for a small course, leaving space to do some

Make your first fence small and encouraging.

Start with the fences low and build up. With a sticky jumper, you can lower a whole course right down to begin with, then get more ambitious as your confidence grows.

By building practice fences that can be jumped safely from either direction (including having a groundline on both sides), you can make the most of the equipment you have.

flat-work schooling too, is about the same in total as a dressage arena (40m x 20m/132ft x 66ft).

● Always remove any cups you aren't using from the stands.

One by one

Don't face your pony with a whole course straight away. Prepare as usual with a little flat-work to loosen up. You may want to do some poles and grids to get in the swing before trying individual fences. Work at linking two or three fences together before tackling a simple course.

If your pony is a sticky jumper who treats every fence as if it might bite him, or a lazy character you find hard to get going, then start off almost at ground level. Raise the fences little by little once he has had a chance to get a good look at each and knows the track. Then he has no excuses!

If, on the other hand, you have a tearaway type, don't be afraid of circling in front of each fence to regain balance and control. Although this is not allowed in competition, it is a valuable steadying and calming exercise at home. There are more hints to help with ponies who rush their fences on pages 60-61.

tip
for the
top

Move jumps around frequently before take-offs and landings get too poached up.

ideas for practice courses

Using four fences *built to be jumped any way*

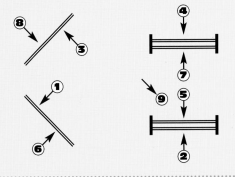

Using three fences *built to be jumped any way*

(version one)

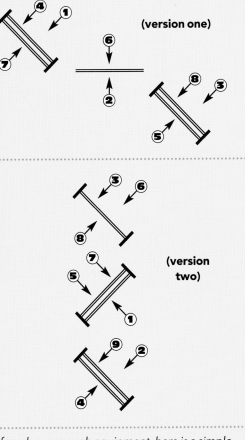

(version two)

If you have enough equipment, here is a simple course to practise at home; try fences 3 & 4 in a figure of eight, then put the whole course together

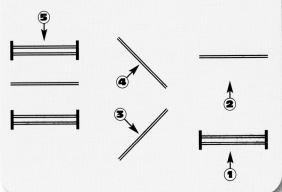

do-it-yourself jumps

How can you perfect your jumping at home when ready-made show jumps cost a fortune? Answer – by making your own! It's simpler and cheaper than you think, and maybe Mum or Dad will help you out. All it takes is a trip down the timber yard, a lick of paint left over from the decorating and a little ingenuity, and you can create an impressive array of training fences from 'junk' without making your paddock look like a scrapyard.

What's more, the pony that has practised over a variety of odd-looking obstacles at home, isn't going to be easily fazed by anything out of the ordinary he may meet in the ring.

All sorts of things can be transformed into jumps – the only rule is that they are solid and they are safe.

poles

● Most timber merchants stock rustic poles you can then paint yourself. Go for poles of even 4in (8cm) diameter, around 10-12ft (3-3.6m) long. Avoid flimsy ones that will knock down or break easily.
● Carpet-roll inner tubes make great poles.
● Drainpipes can be useful, although they are rather light. Fill them with sand so they don't knock down so easily.
● Including some planks will be handy practice. These must have 'handles' fixed on, and sit on flat cups for safety.

stands

● Ideas for DIY jump stands include straw bales, old stable buckets, plastic containers, piles of tyres or traffic cones. Old cones can be picked up at the council depot. Plastic containers once used for chemicals or motor oil can be washed out carefully and filled with sand to weight them down. Beer barrels are safe and solid.

Old empty oil-drums can be bought cheaply from garages, factories and scrapyards. They must be clean, in good condition with no rusty, sharp edges. Clean with a paraffin-soaked rag, sandpaper and paint. Weight down inside for extra stability.
● Remember that whatever you use as a stand must be stable and be fixed, so it cannot cause an accident if a pony knocks into it.
● If Dad or Mum are any good at making things, now is the time to get in their good books! Quite professional-looking, versatile stands can be made using cheaply-bought planks of wood. A height of 4-5ft (1.2-1.5m) will be plenty.
● Search around reclaimed timber yards for cheap offcuts.

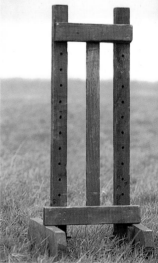

A simple design for a home-made stand – sturdy and safe.

Ask family and friends to check out their sheds for old bits of wood .

● Look how the cups can be built into the stands using blocks of wood or 'slices' of drainpipe (see pictures, right). Ideally, for 4in (8cm) poles, cups should be 4¹/₂-5 ins (9-10cm) across and 1¹/₂ ins (3cm) deep. Planks and fillers should rest on flat cups.

fillers

● Straw bales and traffic cones make excellent DIY fillers. Tuck fern or conifer twigs into the string of straw bales to create a brush-effect. Old tyres are useful, and can be propped up against a pole or hung over one. Most tyre fitters will be happy for you to take a stack away for no charge. Choose a set that are about the same size.

● Plastic sheeting is great to produce a range of fillers that you can swap and change according to the type of fences your pony needs to practise most. Have a few plain sheets for straightforward fences, then make up some spookier ones by painting the sheets in bright colours, patterns or as a wall. Let your imagination run wild!

● Oil-drums can be used upright or on their sides, but should then be made stable using pegs in the ground so they cannot roll.

● When using plastic sheets, secure them firmly by tucking under a pole at the top and the base of the fence.

● Know anyone who has taken down some old doors? Remove the fittings, fix a small bracket on each end to rest on a flat cup, and they make perfect, solid fillers for practising narrow fences.

● Old feed or fertiliser bags stuffed with straw or newspaper and weighted down are safe – and very spooky!

● Sawn-off wooden pallets are useful for filling in, and can be found at factories, industrial sites and transport depots (don't forget to ask the person in charge!). Pallets are best stuffed with twigs or conifer rather than left gappy. Line with hardboard, paint on a brick pattern and hey presto – a wall!

Give your fences a solid appearance by using straw bales as fillers.

If you lay barrels on their sides, remember to secure them with a stake in the ground to prevent rolling.

water trays and ditches

● Use plastic sheeting weighted down or painted hardboard to create a water tray effect underneath fences.

● If possible, dig a shallow ditch somewhere in the practice paddock. You can then build whatever fence you like over the top, and use it either dry or with your 'pretend water' sheet inside.

Left: Old plastic sheeting has lots of uses! Here it's an instant water tray.

more DIY tips

● To create a decent grid or small course, aim to collect or make about 10 poles.

● Don't skimp on fillers. Remember how off-putting and awkward a flimsy, gappy obstacle is for a pony to jump. Always make your fences wide and solid and use proper groundlines.

● Go wild with that paint! The brighter your practice fences, the less chance your pony will be shocked by dazzling colours he may see in the ring.

● For fences to be jumped in either direction, make them look different on each side and double their effect!

● Whatever you use for your jumps, check there are no sharp edges or old nails sticking out that could cause an injury.

● Jumps left in fields can rot, get nibbled and cause accidents. When not in use, bring your fences into a secure place, under cover if possible. Paint wood preserver on fixed rustic fences.

Out with those old buckets! Anything safe you can find to fill in your fences will help prepare your pony to expect the unexpected!

The place to be

When deciding where to put your jumps, AVOID:

● Difficult approaches, such as boggy, rough or sloping ground.

● Squeezing too many jumps into a small area. Allow plenty of space for each approach and landing. Don't place jumps too near to wire fencing or trees.

● Jumping into bright sun, or dark shadows.

● Tricky angles.

Go natural

Include some natural and rustic fences and you can practise cross-country jumping too.

your first show

Even Olympic champions had to enter the ring for their very first nail-biting competitive round once upon a time! Armed with these handy hints, you will get off to a flying start on the show jumping scene.

When and where

Even if you live in an area that's not especially horsey, a little detective work will reveal plenty of small shows suitable for first-timers. The fun needn't end with the summer, either. Shows simply move indoors for the dreary winter months.

Most horsey events include some show jumping for riders of all ages and abilities. The type of small show you will be aiming for may be organised by a local riding centre, riding club or Pony Club. Some are for members only, but many shows are open to all. Look out for adverts in local papers, your tack shop or ask around your pony-owning and riding friends.

Entering

The classes to be held at the show are listed in a programme called a schedule. Read it carefully, including the rules, which can vary from show to show. If entries need to be made before the day, send yours off in good time with the correct fees. At many small shows you can enter on the day, giving you a chance for a sneak preview of the course before parting with your money!

Into the big time!

Once you get bitten by the show jumping bug you can get seriously into the sport by joining the 'professionals' and registering with the BSJA. 'Affiliated' shows have a high standard of course-building and competition, but not all the fences are mountainous. Classes start at 3 ft (90cm) – and you will be rubbing shoulders with the best!

preparation points

Just some of the kit you're going to need for a show. Make a list beforehand so you aren't missing anything on the day.

● Prepare properly by practising at home, but don't overdo it and sour your pony. Investing in lessons with a qualified instructor in the weeks before the show will be money well spent.
● Make sure your pony's shoes will be in good condition for show day, and prepare your trailer or horsebox.
● List the things you will need to take and get them ready beforehand:
– your own riding kit (see page 10), including a short whip (45-75cm)
– pony's tack
– grooming kit & sponges

– headcollar & rope, summer sheet/rug
– water & bucket
– haynet
– first aid kit
– money for entries
– packed lunch

● Set off in good time, especially if you are entering on the day.
● Don't be over-ambitious at first. Choose a class that suits you where you can both have fun.
● Before the class begins, walk the course carefully. 'Ride' through it in your mind several times, thinking through how you will make your turns, the exact strides in any combinations, and noting any difficult or 'spooky' fences that will need stronger riding. Concentrate as you walk – don't chatter to your mates!
● Put your number down on the board in the collecting (warm-up) ring. This will be the order in which the riders then jump, so you will see how much time you have to tack up and work in. As a rough guide, each round takes about 3 minutes at an outdoor show and 2 minutes indoors.

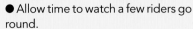

● Allow time to watch a few riders go round.
● Warm your pony up, don't wear him out! Use preparation time to get him listening to you, not to impress the opposition. Walk, trot and canter circles and two or three low practice jumps in each direction is plenty.
● Watch out for other riders. Only jump the practice fence in the correct direction. Don't hog it – everyone would like a go!
● If your pony is gee-d up, relax him with a quiet walk.

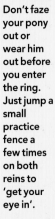

Don't faze your pony out or wear him out before you enter the ring. Just jump a small practice fence a few times on both reins to 'get your eye in'.

Reward your pony with a pat if he has done well.

pony. It takes experience to get a team jumping as well at shows as they can do at home. Excitement and nerves easily make things go wrong – even champions have their off-days! Get back your confidence by popping over a low practice fence once or twice, then resolve to work on your problem back at home.

● Pat your pony and reward him with a loose rein at the end of the round. Do a large circle to steady up before heading for the exit.

● When you have finished, untack and give your pony some water and a rest in the shade. Riding him around all day or using him like an armchair to sit on while you watch the show is very unfair.

ring-time tips

● Use the time before the bell to get in balance with a large circle in canter, on the correct rein ready for the first fence.

● Don't zoom around at 100mph unnecessarily. Remember everything you have learnt! Leaving the fences up is the most important thing.

● If you land on the wrong leg, take your time to come back to trot and ask for canter again.

● Use the space between the fences to help your pony. Ride deep into the corners.

● If your pony has a stop, it is often because he wasn't presented properly at the fence. Do a large circle and try again. Don't just fire him at it from only a few strides away.

● If you are unlucky and are eliminated, don't take your frustration out on your

Wait for the bell before starting. Use this time to get your pony's attention and plan your approach to the first fence.

rules and scoring

Most UK shows are run under British Show Jumping Association (BSJA) rules. In the USA the governing body is the AHSA (American Horse Shows Association).

The most important rules of the ring to remember are:

● Always go through the start and finish flags.

● Wait for the judges to ring the bell before starting. Once you hear the bell, you must begin within 30 seconds.

● If your pony has a refusal and knocks down the fence, wait for the bell before re-attempting it.

● Take the jumps in the correct order. Keep the red flags on your right (remember R=Right!) and white on your left.

● If you have a refusal or run-out in the middle of a combination, you must tackle the whole combination again.

Each round is scored like this:

Knockdown	4 faults
First refusal/run-out/circle	3 faults
Second refusal/run-out/circle	6 faults
Third refusal/run-out/circle	Elimination
Fall or dismount before leaving the ring	Elimination

Enjoy your show – but try to make sure your pony does too!

jump off!

Have a pat on the back when you make it to the jump-off – all that hard work is paying off! A rosette is in sight, but don't let the excitement make you forget the essential rules that will keep you jumping clear all the way to the winning line-up.

Jump-offs are won with skill, not just speed.

What is a jump-off?

The jump-off is show jumping's equivalent of a 'final'. Those riders who have clear rounds go forward to jump against each other in an order drawn by the judges. Depending on the exact rules for that class, the jump-off may simply be over a raised course, or it may also be 'against the clock'. In this case, each rider is timed and the fastest one with the least number of faults wins. Usually the course is based on that used in the first round, with some fences missed out.

In the USA, novice competitors rarely jump against the clock. Young riders, horses and ponies are encouraged to polish up their technique in 'equitation' type classes, judged mainly on style, before being asked to step up the pace.

No speeding!

Many riders lose in a jump-off because they mistakenly think they need to gallop flat out. Timed jump-offs actually call for great skill from the pony and the rider. It is no good zooming around with the fastest time if you have flattened the entire course on the way!

As we found on pages 24-25, nothing is more likely to make a pony hollow and knock down a pole, to get off-balance and grind to a halt, or to take off badly, than rushing. By all means get your pony moving on a bit. But aim to tackle the jump-off fences exactly as usual – with balance, bounce and an even beat. Novice riders should concentrate on a steady round in a nice rhythm rather than tearing about and making mistakes. A slow, clear round often gets in the ribbons – and can even win the day.

tip for the top

Everything happens so fast in jump-offs that it is easy to get carried away. Don't get forwards too early before your fences. Be ready to sit up and drive on if your pony hesitates.

Whooah! Even though you have upped the pace, to avoid disasters you still have to remember that A B C for every approach!

Seconds out

But if you aren't using much more speed, how do you get around any faster? The answer is, the way you ride between the fences. This is done by:
– turning
– taking jumps on an angle
– using fewer strides

Jump-offs are usually won by super-obedient horses and ponies that save seconds by turning quickly and in balance, and jumping accurately from a relatively short approach to a fence. These are all skills that take practice at home.

tip for the top

Don't forget to push on through the finish!

Turning

● Study the plan of the jump-off course carefully and plan your route according to your pony's ability.
● Cut corners and trim turns where you can, but don't ask the impossible! It is no use if your pony loses all his 'go' and hasn't time to see the fence properly.
● Avoid losing impulsion around your turns by using plenty of inside leg. Don't forget that outside rein and outside leg though. The outside rein will steady the pony so he does not

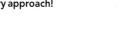

Practise tight but balanced turns at home.

hurry and get too much weight on to his fore-hand. Your outside leg keeps his quarters bending round the turn instead of trailing out.

● Look for the next fence before you start turning – in fact, immediately you land .

● Try to land on the correct leading leg for the next fence. As you go over, feel the rein on the side of the leading leg you will want, and give a little nudge with your heel on this side.

Angles

Cut in too short to a fence and you risk a glance-off

● Novice ponies and riders should still aim to approach each fence centrally. More experienced partnerships, however, can try taking some fences on an angle, especially if a tight turn is needed on landing.

● Don't make the angle too shallow or you will risk a glance-off.

● Indicate the way you plan to turn afterwards by shifting your weight very slightly that way and squeezing with the inside rein as you go over.

● Avoid jumping spreads at a sharp angle. A 3ft spread could quickly become a 6ft one!

● Always get straight for combinations.

Taking strides out

● Work at the exercises on page 35 to make your pony respond quickly when you ask for fewer, longer, strides. This way you can reduce the number of strides needed between fences without going any faster.

● Don't throw the reins away and lose contact or the pony will go 'flat'.

● Never lengthen the stride in front of a fence if you are planning to make a sharp turn on landing.

try this

four square

This grid is great for sharpening up ponies and riders. Set up four small fences to make a square, with two strides distance between each side. One can be a spread (a parallel, so it can be jumped either way). Work in and out and through the square, turning a different way each time (get the correct leading leg!)

try this

in between

Set up a small parallel of cross-poles, with another three canter strides away (preferably against the long side of the school or a wall). Three placing poles (the closest set at 11-12ft/3.3-3.6m) will help establish a rhythm at first, then can be removed. Work straight through the grid, A to B, a few times. Now try coming in between the two jumps, taking

Work round in a figure of eight, landing, turning and coming in again.

fence B first. On landing, take a wide semicircle around and, heading in the other direction, take fence A. Work around in a figure of eight, landing, turning and cutting in to the next fence. Gradually try to reduce the number of strides in your turn, creating a U-turn rather than a semicircle. Practise on both reins.

try this

side by side

Set up two low fences side by side. Put a cone or other marker between the two, a distance away, in both directions. First in trot and then in canter, practise jumping one fence, turning around the marker, then jumping the other. Go around in a circle, trying to land on the correct leg each time. Use two low uprights at first, then progress to include one, and then two, spreads.

● Look to the next fence.

● Keep each turn balanced using lots of inside leg and enough outside hand and leg.

● Keep plenty of bounce in your canter, but think rhythm (shout 'bounce, bounce, bounce' out loud!)

● Don't hurry your pony on. Wait for each fence to come to you!

Aim for the next fence as you land. More inside leg would have stopped this pony 'motorbiking' the turn.

● Each approach, look for a spot about 6ft (1.8m) in front of each fence, allowing you to be straight for the last stride.

● Turn your head to look for the next fence as you land, not once you have gone around the corner.

● Avoid tipping forward and 'firing' your pony at the fence. To get a balanced turn that keeps its energy, you will need to sit up a little. See above for turning tips.

● Aim for a good active rhythm all the way, regaining it as quickly as possible after each landing.

● As you get the hang of things, try asking your pony to turn very slightly on his take-off stride. This is the start of learning to turn in the air – a trick the experts use to stunning effect.

● Try to take as few strides as possible around each turn, without losing rhythm or impulsion.

The fences go up in the jump-off, but don't lose your cool!

cross-country
class

Here we go!

Once in the swing of show jumping, most of you will probably be itching to try some cross-country jumping. Whoa! Don't gallop off before learning about the differences between show jumping in an arena and facing the fences of a cross-country course.

Spot the difference

The basic rules of good jumping that we have learned so far remain just as important in cross-country as they are in show jumping. But you and your pony will have to adapt your technique between and over the fences to suit the different questions that a cross-country course asks. Take a look at the main differences between the two 'disciplines':

the fences

Show jumping:
● Fences are generally brightly-painted and artificial-looking.
● Poles and fillers knock down easily.
● Courses contain around 10-12 fences with short distances between and lots of turns.
● Timing is only really important in a jump-off against the clock.

Cross-country:
● Fences are 'natural', either made of rustic materials or using features of the landscape, e.g. hedges, logs and banks.
● Ups and downs, plus in and out of water, feature in most courses.
● The fences are solid and do not knock down (although they are made to be taken apart quickly if necessary).
● A course can have 20-30 fences, with long gallops in between.
● Most courses are timed, or include a timed section.

riding the course

Show jumping:
● The rider has only a short time after each fence to reorganise and plan her next approach.
● A short, bouncy canter is crucial, to get a very rounded shape over each fence. The rider aims to contain the pony's energy so he is like a 'coiled spring'.

Cross-country:
● Keeping rhythm, balance and impulsion all the way around the course, with its long gallops, unusual fences and changes of direction and level, is much more difficult than in an arena.
● The fences are very solid-looking. Some are designed to catch out less courageous ponies and riders. The rider has to be extra-bold and confident.

Cross-country jumping takes you up and down hills, through woods and water, and over all kinds of natural obstacles. It's brilliant fun!

tip for the top

Practise opening out into cross-country canter then coming back to a bouncier, show jumping canter in the school or out on hacks.

In cross-country, the rider stays in a forward position between the fences. This way she can keep her weight off the pony's back, but still leg him forwards in a fast but balanced canter. She is ready to sit down and drive if he hesitates before a fence.

tip for the top

A pony cannot jump well from a flat-out gallop! Even if you are going fast, aim to ride your pony forwards 'from behind'. Think of his hindquarters as his engine. Use your legs to create power, but contain it with your rein contact. Then your pony will be light in front, ready for take-off.

● The rider must be able to adjust her approach to suit many different types of obstacle (see next page) and terrain.
● Balance and rhythm are as crucial as in an arena, but the pace is faster.
● Although the pony still rounds over a fence, he has to gallop on swiftly afterwards, so he makes less of an 'up and over' shape over the fence and more of an 'out and over' shape.

up to and over the fences

Show jumping:
● In the approach, the rider is slightly forward out of the saddle, ready to take up jump position as the pony takes off.

Cross-country:
● The rider is slightly more upright in the approach, placed a fraction behind the centre of balance, in order to push the pony on more easily if necessary.
● Over the fence, the basic jumping position is the same, but your lower leg hugs the pony's sides slightly further forward than usual. This more secure position means, in an emergency, you have plenty of leg in front of you and will not tip forwards so easily.
● Even if you get behind the movement, try not to pull on the mouth. A pony that is constantly restricted or jabbed over his fences will jump bunched up and get himself into trouble. He will soon lose confidence and start to refuse.

getting in gear

Kitted out for cross-country.

Even though you won't be facing Badminton-sized fences just yet, aim for a jumping position as balanced and steady as this one. Look how the rider's leg is well forwards underneath her for security. Although she is maintaining a contact on the reins, the horse has all the freedom he needs to stretch his neck.

A stronger bit or noseband may be needed for ponies whose enthusiasm gets the better of them. But remember, many only pull if their riders pull back! Check out pages 60-61 for help with speedsters.

The extra speed and risk of cross-country add to the thrills – but also the spills! Be prepared to have fun but stay as safe as possible by getting in the correct gear:

Rider: Helmet up to highest approved standard – jumper or sweatshirt in your cross-country colours – silk hat cover to match – body protector – jodhpurs – short or long boots – short whip – gloves – stock (hunting tie).

Pony: Protective boots, or carefully-fitted exercise bandages on all four legs – martingale/breastplate – surcingle around saddle for extra security – stronger bit/noseband if necessary.

As you land over one fence, look up and ride positively for the next.

fence by fence across country

The fence may be small, but jumping from the bright light into a shady wood could easily faze your pony.

Galloping and jumping cross-country is one of the biggest thrills on horseback. But if you want to turn that fun into clear rounds and prizes, you will need to do some homework. Schooling over a variety of fences like the ones you could meet in a cross-country event will mean you and your pony are ready for anything!

Shady situation

● Horses find it tricky to adjust to jumping from the light into shadows, so be ready for your pony to think twice.
● Even if the jump itself is low and innocent-looking, the situation will seem suspicious to a newcomer to natural fences.
● Look ahead, sit up and ride on strongly.
● Keep a steady contact on the reins.

Dealing with ditches

● Ditches can be placed in front of, underneath or after a fence, or may be by themselves (called an 'open ditch'). Rails followed by an open ditch then more rails is known as a 'coffin'.
● If you have a stop at an open ditch, don't turn away. Keep at your pony until he walks over it.

tip for the top

Polish up your cross-country performance by hiring a purpose-built course in your area. Take your instructor along for help and advice.

Don't dither at ditches! Look up and ride on strongly.

● As long as you take off with enough power, a ditch behind a fence is not too difficult as the pony's jump will carry him over.

● A ditch in front of or below a fence (a 'trakehner'), makes it look enormous! Try to forget it's there – look up, ride on positively and think how small it really is!

● Don't approach flat out, but use your legs strongly once you know he has seen the ditch. Be prepared for the pony to have second thoughts as his eyes are drawn down to it. Beware of dropping your contact at the last minute.

Upright answers

Treat vertical uprights such as walls, gates and rails with caution. Come down to more of a show jumping pace as you approach. Aim for maximum bounce.

Drop it!

● A fence or step where the ground on landing is lower than on take-off is called a 'drop'. From on foot, drops often look like the Grand Canyon. But ride in confidently and your pony will think little of them.

● Avoid bowling in on a long, fast stride – you will either risk a stop when your pony suddenly sees his landing spot disappear, or else be shot into orbit! Approach with energy and in a balanced rhythm, giving time for your pony to see what's coming.

● Eyes up, looking to the next fence, not down in the undergrowth!

● If the drop is not too steep, lean forwards slightly, in balance, with your lower leg well underneath you. Don't get too far forwards though – be ready to sit up right away on landing.

● If the drop is steep, sit right back and slip the reins.

Accuracy is the key to jumping corners and V-fences. Even if you decide on the in-and-out option rather than risk the corner, you must plan a line and go for it!

Cutting corners

● Accuracy is the key to clearing any kind of corner or combination fence. Concentrate hard on a straight, bouncy, balanced approach, almost show jumping style. Look up!

● Pick the line you are going to use when walking the course – then stick to it! Choose a line not too far in (where the spread widens), or too close to the corner end (where you risk a run-out).

● Focusing on a point ahead, such as a tree, can help.

● When schooling novice ponies, use a wing on the corner.

● Only attempt to jump the corner itself if you have had plenty of practice. At first, go for an accurate jump in, stride and jump out.

● Think about the level of the ground – a sloping approach will carry you into the fence faster.

Making a splash

● Most ponies enjoy water once they have been carefully introduced to it.

● It is usually best to go for a brisk trot into and through water. The straighter leg action makes cantering through water much harder for your pony.

● Sit well back on the approach, with your lower leg underneath you. Ride on strongly but keep the rein contact. You are aiming to push your pony's quarters underneath him but still keep him light in front.

● Sit well up for a drop down into water. Get upright as quickly as possible on landing, ready to ride forwards.

● Be ready to use one hand to pick up the pony's head as you land, especially if the water is quite deep.

● Start a novice pony off by going into and out of water on a gentle slope and using a more experienced pony to give a lead.

Leg on and be ready to give with your hands for all steps up, including those out of water. You need to get near enough to the step so you don't finish up 'belly-flopping' on to it.

Practise opening your fingers to 'slip' the reins over a drop fence, or if you ever get left behind. This avoids jabbing the pony in the mouth and gives him freedom to use his head and neck to balance. Gather the reins up quickly after landing for a controlled get-away.

problem-

Are you fed up with run-outs and refusals? Does your pony behave like the 8.30 express train – or have all the impulsion of a garden snail? Perhaps he always misses out on the jump-off by getting four faults every round. Or scatters poles around the paddock without a care in the world. Whatever your jumping problem, these troubleshooting pages hope to provide some helpful hints on tackling common sticky situations.

Why do things go wrong?

Every pony jumps differently. Some enjoy it; they are very willing and have a naturally good technique, making life easy for their riders. Others are far less obliging; they are always ready to take advantage or keep their riders working every step of the way. Sometimes, as we will see below, ponies can have a good reason to be awkward.

But don't forget – it takes two to make a team. Whatever pony you are on, remember the golden rule we learnt on page 5. It is the rider's job to get the pony to each fence in a way that should make it easier to take off and clear it than it is to stop, run out or knock it down. Ninety per cent of the time, jumping problems can be traced to rider errors, particularly in the approach to the fence.

First things first

Before looking at what the rider can do to avoid silly mistakes or to improve their own and their pony's style, cast an eye down this checklist of things that will be certain to put any pony, however keen or willing, off jumping. If you are having difficulties, particularly if they have come on suddenly, could any of these apply to you?

Is your pony uncomfortable?
Check: The fit of his tack – the bit you are using – his feet and legs – his back – whether his teeth need rasping – you are not jabbing him in the mouth – you are not bumping down on to his back on landing – the ground is suitable for jumping, i.e. not too soft and slippery, hard, or uneven.

Are you, or your pony, nervous, afraid or confused?
Check: Your pony has had enough basic training in jumping – you are not trying jump fences that are too big or difficult – neither of you have had a previous bad experience – the fence itself and the ground are both safe and suitable – other conditions are not off-putting or distracting (e.g. high winds or hot weather) – you are giving clear, correct and positive aids he can have confidence in.

Is your pony tired or fed up?
Check: He is fit – he is healthy and getting enough of the right type of food – you are not pushing him too far – you haven't soured him with too much jumping – he simply doesn't enjoy jumping and would rather be doing something else.

If your checklist comes up to scratch, the chances are the problem lies in the way you are riding up and over the fence.

Don't ask too much of your pony.

refusals and run-outs

Sooner or later every rider finds themselves on a pony who refuses a jump. Refusals and run-outs (where the pony runs past the fence) are two of the most common problems for novice ponies and riders. If your pony consistently refuses, first of all, look again at the causes above.

All ponies have the odd stop, and there can be many varied reasons. A different one might apply each occasion it happens, or you could be repeating the same mistake every time. Sometimes it is hard to work out the reason. However, the pony often gives clues in the way the refusal happens. Over the next few pages we will look at some different examples.

Sharp edges to the teeth are just one reason why a pony may be unhappy about jumping. Have teeth checked twice yearly.

solving

Be patient when attempting to overcome problems – your hard work will pay off in the end

trouble-shooting tips

● Whatever your difficulty, it will take time, patience and plenty of homework to resolve. Accept that show plans may need to be put on hold for a while until there are no mishaps in your practice sessions.

● Never expect a refusal. Your pony will sense it and oblige!

When your pony stops, don't be in too much of a hurry to turn away. Lower the fence right down, then INSIST he goes over it.

● If your pony stops, don't let him off too easily! Only turn away if the fence is too big to jump from a standstill, otherwise refusing will become a habit. Keep at him until he steps or hops over (be prepared for what may be an awkward leap!). If you have a problem with a particular fence in a jumping session, lower it right down until it is small enough for him to step over – then insist he does. Then you can gradually work back up again.

● Being careful is not necessarily a bad thing – the best show jumpers are a little bit cautious and will back off their fences slightly to weigh each one up. What's important is that your pony trusts you and responds to your aids. He must 'think forwards', so when you say "Yes, go!", he goes!

● Are you pals with your pony? Who is in charge? Sometimes the way you get on together can be partly to blame for refusals. A pony that takes no notice of his owner when she is handling or riding him from day to day, or who often has his own way or gets away with naughty behaviour, is likely to think he can take advantage when it comes to jumping too. Find out more about handling and riding a pony the right way in the Understanding Ponies book in this series.

Are you pals with your pony? How the two of you get on can make a lot of difference to your performance.

to smack, or not to smack?

There is no denying that some ponies will try to get away with putting as little effort as possible into jumping. But don't be too hasty to smack a pony to make him jump as he will soon ignore your leg aids and only jump if the whip is used.

Even a smack as punishment for a refusal can do more harm than good. Are you sure he didn't have a reasonable excuse for stopping, or that the mistake wasn't yours?

If you are 100 per cent certain the pony is being deliberately naughty, make him stand in front of the fence or grid, lowering it right down if need be. Keep using your legs to ask him to go forwards over it. Only use your whip – quickly and firmly, but calmly – if he tries to turn himself away.

For your pony to understand any punishment, it must be given immediately (within three seconds) after the exact bad behaviour that has caused it. Turning your pony away from a fence yourself, then smacking him for the refusal as you canter off, will only leave him totally confused! What did he do wrong – the turn, or the canter? The refusal will be a distant memory!

After a naughty refusal over larger fences or in the ring, give one firm smack behind the girth, straight away in front of the fence. Then concentrate on riding a careful, determined approach next time.

my pony won't even go near the jumps

problem 1

What's going on:

Well-trained ponies rarely refuse to approach a fence altogether, unless they are worried, either by its particularly unusual appearance or for some other reason (see previous page). If there is nothing obviously off-putting about the fence, it can usually be traced to lack of training, i.e. the pony doesn't know what is expected of him. Sometimes an older pony can simply be nappy (check out the Understanding Ponies book in this series for ideas on dealing with nappy ponies).

Your aim is:

To make sure your pony is always prepared for what you ask him to do and confident about having a go at it.

● Go right back to basics with training, both on the flat and jumping. Only progress step by step once your pony is happy and willing.
● Always ride positively, concentrating on a good technique and getting plenty of impulsion.
● Introduce new questions gradually. Build up the height and difficulty of fences slowly. If necessary, make a gap in the middle of the jump that the pony can walk through. Then place a pole there, and build up from here.
● Don't jump too often, over-face or rush a pony, particularly a youngster.
● Build small (safe) versions of spooky or unusual fences at home to practise before going to an event or show. Include

Whenever you come up against major problems, the answer lies in going right back to the beginning and getting the basics right.

particular problem fences in your grids.
● A very unwilling or easily-scared pony is unlikely ever to give you much jumping fun. Think seriously about either sticking to other activities you can enjoy together, or selling him on to a non-jumping home and finding another pony.

A pony who is 'backing off' a fence needs strong, determined riding to boost his confidence.

my pony gradually grinds to a halt in front of the fence

problem 2

What's going on:

Sometimes a pony actually puts the brakes on (called 'backing off') as he nears a fence because he is worried about it and is being over-cautious. Or he could simply get slower and slower because he is running out of impulsion, and by the time he gets up to the fence doesn't have enough 'oomph' to take off. This may be down to deliberate laziness or riding that is not strong or positive enough.

Keep fences low in your schooling sessions and introduce anything new or spooky gradually. Fillers can be included as wings to start with, then moved little by little into the centre of the fence.

Your aim is:

a) To boost his confidence generally, so he is happy to trust you and tackle whatever comes his way.

● Never over-face yourself or your pony. Work on the basics over simple, low grids and inviting fences. Only move up in height or difficulty once your pony is completely confident with no sign of hesitation.
● Ride positively, really driving forwards and 'attacking' each fence or exercise. Don't get forwards too early before the fence or tip forwards if the pony starts to slow down. Keep a deep seat, using strong aids and even your voice to encourage your pony (but do not shout at him).
● If you feel hesitation, give a quick tap down the shoulder, without taking your hands off the reins.
● Keep a contact right up to the fence, but try not to fiddle with the reins. Watch that you are not giving contradictory aids by mistake – i.e. kicking on with your heels, but pulling on the reins at the same time.
● Use placing poles and the other basic exercises in this book to develop balance and a good, confidence-building rhythm.
● If spookiness is your pony's problem, incorporate one brightly coloured pole (or filler, if that is what worries him) into a grid. Vary its placing to keep him guessing!

❓ problem 3 my pony goes on towards the fence, then slams on the brakes at the very last minute

What's going on:

In this case, something has usually gone wrong with the approach. Arriving at the fence, the pony finds he isn't organised enough to take off. The rider may have cut in too sharply or at an angle. The pony could have got out of rhythm or balance and ended up on a bad stride. The rider may have interfered too much and put him off. Or he may have rushed in too fast, arrived completely flat and too 'stretched out'.

Look for the reason for a last-minute stops.

Your aim is:

To get a good approach every time, giving your pony the best chance of arriving well set up:

● Basic exercises on the flat and over poles and grids will improve activity, balance, rhythm and straightness.
● Plan ahead and stay on the ball. When schooling, if something isn't right, circle so you can have a better go next time round.
● As soon as you land over a fence, look ahead to the next to see your 'line'.
● Always come in at a sensible pace. Remember – you want energy, not speed! If your pony rushes, try the tips on page 60-61.
● Keep your legs on to create impulsion, but contain it with a consistent rein contact or the pony will become unbalanced and too much 'on his forehand'.
● Keep your body and hands still, interfering as little as possible.
● Practise at home over the more scary-looking obstacles.

Use poles and simple grid exercises to help develop balance and confidence-boosting rhythm.

Dawdling won't do. You're the driver!

b) To ride positively and create enough impulsion for take-off.

● Concentrate! Always ride with determination and commitment so your pony is convinced that you are convinced! This is true for every pony and every approach, but particularly so for cheeky or lazy characters who are reluctant to make the effort.
● Before tackling fences, start each jumping session working on exercises to improve your pony's responsiveness and impulsion (see pages 24-25). This means flat-work!
● Get your pony's attention before starting the approach so he knows you mean business and that there is about to be some action!
● Take care not to let the energy you create with your legs disappear out the front end by not having an even, constant contact on the pony's mouth.

❓ problem 4 my pony often puts in a little extra stride in front of the fence, so he gets too close and takes off awkwardly or stops

What's going on:

Sudden braking or putting in a short stride (called 'propping') can happen when the rider takes her legs off and drops the reins at the last, crucial moment. The pony thinks the rider has given up, and so has second thoughts. Sometimes the rider has come forwards into jump position too early, so, as the pony hesitates, she falls on to the neck making it impossible for him to take off. Or she carries on over the fence by herself! Sore feet can also be a cause of propping.

Dropping the contact just before the fence is very unnerving for the pony.

Your aim is:

To keep riding right up to the fence. To wait for the fence instead of anticipating the take-off.

● Keep a steady, even contact (put a sticky-tape marker on each rein in the place you are aiming to hold it).
● Have your legs close to the pony's sides all the way. Ride as if you mean it!
● Try to relax and breathe deeply and evenly. Look up beyond the fence.
● Focus on getting a good rhythm rather than worrying about when or if the pony will take off (see pages 28-29). Work with grids and placing poles to boost your confidence.
● Put a take-off pole on the ground about 1ft (30cm) in front of the fence to encourage the pony to stand back.

Avoid hustling your pony into a fence and risking a stop or awkward last stride.

problem 5

my pony likes jumping and rarely refuses, but often knocks poles down

What's going on?

As before, it's all in the approach. Arriving too close to a fence means the pony will often hit it with his forelegs as he comes up. Taking off too far away or without enough impulsion means the hindlegs could hit the fence as he comes down. Not enough activity in the approach, too much speed or a rider with restricting hands means the pony can jump flat or with a hollow instead of a rounded shape. Some ponies will naturally try to be careful and others appear not to care less if they hit a pole, but the more careless ones can be improved.

Your aim is:

To forget speed for now, and work on style, accuracy and concentration.

● Use poles, grids and other basic exercises at home to encourage rhythm, balance, agility and neatness. Grids are particularly useful, as they make the pony concentrate on the job! Keep the fences low but varied. Use placing poles to encourage a good outline and even stride. Gradually shorten the distance between the pole and fence so he has to take off closer.

● A grid of bounces is excellent for tidying a pony's style. Also, use lots of small parallels, gradually increasing the spread to make your pony use himself.

A grid of bounces is brilliant for sharpening up a careless pony.

● Work to improve your pony's suppleness and obedience on the flat so it is easier to get him into a rounded outline and listening to you on your approaches to fences.

● Use short spells of flat-work in your jumping sessions to settle him and get his concentration back.

● On your approaches, sit still but ride positively. Aim for balance, rhythm and activity but not speed. Make approaches accurate and straight.

● Keep your hands low but with an even steady contact. Give with the hands as the pony takes off so he is free to stretch his head and neck.

● If the pony tends to trail a particular foreleg, set up a grid of cross-pole bounces, where the poles on that side are set slightly higher than on the other.

Does your pony usually get too close, and knock the fence in front? Or does he take off too far away, and catch it behind?

❓ my pony often runs out or jumps to one side

problem 6

What's going on:

The approach has not been straight, or has been too short for the pony to prepare himself properly. Perhaps he was allowed to drift and is too temptingly close to the side of the fence! Or the rider may have leant to one side and unbalanced him. Maybe the pony has come in too fast, flat and unbalanced, so he can go where he chooses.

Your aim is:

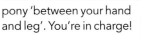

tip for the top

If your pony runs out to the left, correct it by turning to the right and vice versa.

To plan each approach so it is balanced, straight and controlled. To stay in charge!

● Even in a jump-off, give your pony a fair chance. Allow time and space for good approaches.

● Aim for the centre of the fence. Approach straight every time (unless you are practising taking fences at an angle for jump-offs).

● Sit straight and avoid tipping to one side. Look ahead and up. Keep an even contact on both reins – don't be tempted to haul on the inside rein to pull him back on track.

● If the pony often drifts, keep your whip in the hand he tends to go towards. Tap him down his shoulder if you feel him going that way. Keep a good contact on your outside hand and use lots of leg, especially on that side.

● Lay two poles on the ground to act as 'tram lines' to guide you in to a line of poles or a grid.

● School over cross-poles and small fences with 'drop' poles placed at an angle to help guide the pony into the centre.

● Always ride in a straight line away from the fence so the pony doesn't get into the habit of veering off whichever way he chooses.

● Don't come in too fast! Keep a steady pace with the pony 'between your hand and leg'. You're in charge!

If straightness is your problem, set up angled poles on the ground, or 'drop' poles to funnel your pony in.

❓ my pony gets very excited about jumping and rushes at his fences

problem 7

What's going on?

Speeding ponies make mistakes, because they are not listening to their riders. A frantic pony that hurls himself at every fence can look like he is having a great time, but may not be at all. Discomfort and fear can make ponies rush, or they may in fact be worried and want to get it all over with as quickly as possible. Some characters do simply find the whole business of jumping incredibly exciting. Even so, getting away with it shows disobedience and lack of training. Often the rider can make things worse by riding too aggressively, or thinking it is cool to wind their pony up.

It's going to take time to convince your speeding pony to slow down and think about what he is doing.

Your aim is:

To encourage the relaxed and sensible attitude to jumping that gets clear rounds and means everyone enjoys it and stays safe. First:

● Check out possible causes of pain or worry (see page 54).

● Is your pony getting enough time turned out in the field? Are you feeding him too much high-energy food?

● Anxiety can make ponies rush, especially youngsters. Go back to basics and progress step by step to boost confidence.

● Veteran speedsters will take time and patience to convince about slowing down. A stronger bit may be needed to help put you back in control until things improve (see below).

a stronger bit?

Dashing off to buy a stronger bit for a pony that rushes is not necessarily an instant answer. A pony who is actually worried about jumping could be put off even more that way. The excitable type could become more of a jack-in-the-box if he is stopped from going forwards by rough hands and a severe bit or restricting 'gadgets'.

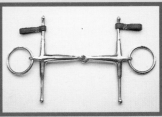

A bit with cheeks, such as this Fulmer snaffle, can help with steering problems.

However, it is important that you are safe and in control. You also need to be able to use your legs effectively, so your pony knows that leg on means "more impulsion", not "go faster". So you may need some help with braking until all the hard work you are putting into schooling starts to take effect! Ask your instructor's advice on any changes of tack that may help.

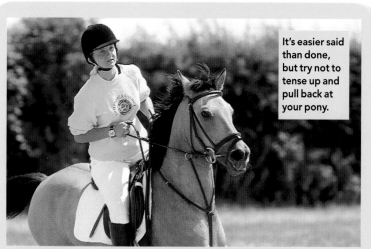

It's easier said than done, but try not to tense up and pull back at your pony.

Remember to have fun!

tips for tanks

think calm

● Try to relax yourself and not to tense up when jumping.

● However keen your pony seems, you must still ride to the fences, so that you are in control. Sit lightly in the saddle but keep your legs wrapped around his sides so you can use them. But make sure you are not over-riding your pony and driving him forwards too fast and onto his forehand.

● Avoid holding on too tightly or constantly pulling, especially if he tends to fight the bit. Allow your arms to move so you can keep a steady but flexible contact instead of hanging on and giving him something to pull against.

● Talk (or sing?) to your pony and rub his neck to help calm him.

● Focus on rhythm. When trotting, slow your sitting and rising right down to help steady him. Use half-halts (see page 25).

insist!

● If you want things to improve, make a resolution *never* to allow your pony to speed into any exercise or fence. If he gets silly at any time when you are schooling, either walk around or do some flat-work until he is calm. He must learn that he will only be allowed to jump when he approaches the pole/grid/fence sensibly.

Insist he is only allowed to go on through the poles or grid when he is prepared to go sensibly.

● Don't fire your pony at any pole, grid or fence from miles away. Come in on a shallow arc so he is balanced but doesn't have time to pick up too much speed. Keep him guessing, so he is never quite sure what you are going to ask next – then he has to listen, not dictate matters himself.

● Work over lots of single fences rather than one after another.

● Keep fences small so that, if necessary, you can walk to within a few strides and then simply allow the pony forwards into trot.

Hands up who's guilty of 'firing' their pony at his fences?

go slow

try this

● Whizz-kid ponies can never do enough work over poles on the ground. These can be placed at random around the paddock, or put in a line or even on a circle. Walk your pony around and between the poles. If he is quiet, then walk over them. Move on to trotting around and then over the poles if he is being sensible.

● Work on small grids, using placing poles in front of the first fence and between fences in the grid. Use bounce and one-stride distances.

● Only allow your pony to go forwards into the grid if he approaches it calmly. Always be ready, if he gets silly, to either circle away or to halt in front of the poles or grid, then allow him forwards when he is quiet. If he gets in a tizz, go back to pole or flat-work for a while.

● Leave courses until this medicine is starting to work. Set up a few small single fences using placing poles in front. Approach off a shallow circle, walking until the last few strides, then moving forwards to trot. Return to walk after landing. Again, if your pony rushes, circle away until the approach is calm.

● When you go on to schooling over combinations and courses, try not to pick up speed between fences. At first, come back to trot after each to re-balance, and circle if you need to. Later, use a steadying pole 18-21ft (5.4-6.3m) after each fence. Use half-halts to stop your pony rushing off. Aim for a smooth flow and even rhythm.

time to think

This grid is designed to make rushing ponies steady up, think and learn to be careful. It is made up of a small parallel cross-pole followed one non-jumping stride on by a single cross-pole followed by another parallel cross-pole one stride on. Each fence has a placing pole midway between. Three poles on the ground are placed in a fan going into the first fence, from both directions, and away from the final fence, in both directions. These are set at 10-12ft apart.

Approach using the poles, as steadily as possible (walk if necessary). At the end of the line of fences, turn alternate ways each time, over the ground poles. These will help you stay steady and re-balance.

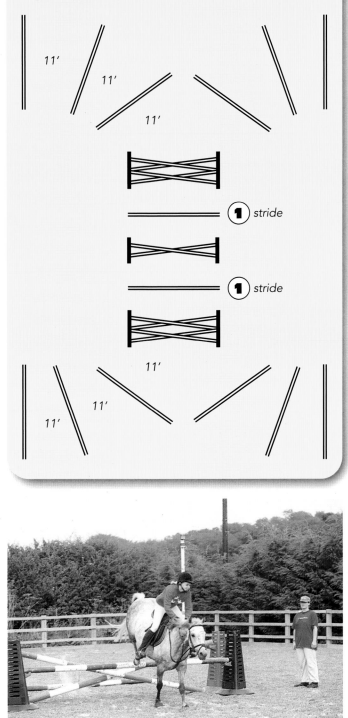

Keep your smarty-pants pony guessing!

which way next?

Some smart ponies think they are so clever at jumping they tank towards any fence they catch sight of. Convince them to listen to you by practising over lots of varied courses. Give the 'which way next' grid a try. Set up three small cross-poles (upright — upright — parallel) at bounce distances, followed after three strides by three small uprights in a fan shape (one directly ahead, the others at a slight angle either side of it). Now choose to head for a different one every time you complete the grid – but be prepared! This exercise is great because it can be ridden from any direction, or the fences can be changed to a mix of spreads and uprights.

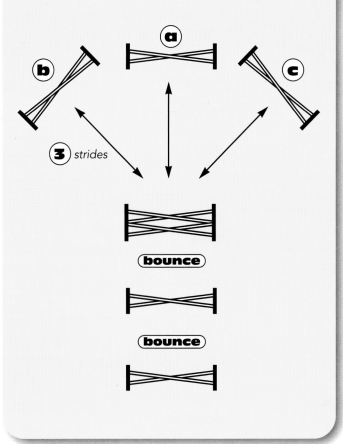

Work through your problems with the help of a specialist instructor.

glossary

The X-shape of a **cross pole** helps guide you into the central, lowest part of the jump.

AHSA American Horse Shows Association, the governing body of the sport of show jumping in the United States.

AGAINST THE CLOCK A show jumping round that is being timed, so that the fastest rider with the least amount of penalties wins.

AIDS Signals the rider uses to communicate with the pony.

APPROACH The way the pony comes in towards the fence.

BASCULE The rounded shape made by the pony's neck and back when he takes a jump correctly.

BELL Sound made by a bell or buzzer to indicate the rider can start their round in a show jumping competition.

BOUNCE When the pony lands and then takes off again over another fence without taking a non-jumping canter stride in between.

BSJA British Show Jumping Association, the governing body of show jumping in the United Kingdom. At shows "affiliated" to the BSJA, riders must be members to take part.

CAVALETTI Type of low schooling fence made up of a pole fixed to an X-shaped stand at either end. Not often seen these days.

CLEAR ROUND When the pony and rider complete a course of jumps without picking up any penalties for fences knocked down, refusals or run-outs.

COFFIN A cross-country fence with three elements – an upright followed by an open ditch, and another upright.

CONTACT Pressure on the reins, creating communication between the rider and the pony's mouth.

COMBINATION A group of two or three fences set at one or two canter strides apart, usually in a straight line. The elements are labelled A, B and C.

COLLECTED A term used to describe a pace, such as trot or canter, where the pony is 'gathered up' by the rider and is stepping right underneath his body with his hindlegs.

CROSS-POLE Fence built by placing two poles at an angle to form a X-shape. An ideal schooling fence, as it helps the pony stay central.

Use **fillers** to make your jumps more solid-looking and get your pony used to the brightly-coloured fences he will face in the ring.

CUPS Shallow, half-circle shaped supports used to rest the fence poles on. Planks must be supported on flat cups.

DISTANCE The space between two fences or elements of a grid or combination.

DOUBLE A combination made up of two fences.

ELEMENT An obstacle that is one of a series in a grid or combination.

EVENTING Horse sport involving three phases of competition – dressage, cross-country and show jumping. Also known as 'horse trials'.

FILLER Painted board supported by low stands used to 'fill in' the base of a fence.

FLAGS In jumping competitions, fences in use are marked with a flag on each side. The flags indicate which direction the fence is to be approached – the red flag is always on the rider's right and the white flag on her left.

FLAT-WORK Ridden training that does not involve jumping.

FLIGHT The moments when the pony is in the air over the fence and none of his feet are touching the ground.

GRID A schooling exercise where a series of small fences and poles on the ground are laid out in a line one after the other with set distances in between to help the pony take off correctly.

GROUNDLINE A way of helping the pony to assess the height of a fence and his distance away from it as he approaches, so he can judge his take-off point accurately. Any part of the fence that touches the ground, eg. a pole or plank at the base of the fence, a pole at an angle resting on the ground, or a filler, provides a ground-line. The ground-line should always be either just in front or directly underneath the front of the fence, never set back.

HOG'S BACK A spread fence built using three sets of wings. The middle pole is the highest, with the front and back poles lower.

HUNTER TRIAL Cross-country jumping competition. Obstacles are those likely to be met out on a day's hunting – eg hedges, timbers, ditches etc, and may include opening and shutting a gate.

IMPULSION Energy, created in the hindquarters by the rider using her legs to make the pony step further underneath his body. Keeping a constant contact on the reins stops the energy being lost out the front end (leading to speed only) and makes the pace active and bouncy, ideal for jumping from.

JUMP-OFF The 'final' of a show jumping class, often 'against the clock'.

MINIMUS Novice jumping class, sometimes called a 'clear round' class. All competitors who jump a clear round get a rosette.

OPEN DITCH A ditch with no fence over the top of it.

OUTLINE The shape made by the pony as he moves. A well-balanced and supple pony that is accepting the rider's contact on the reins and working actively with his hindquarters makes a rounded outline, flexing at his poll so his nose is in line with the ground. A stiff, unbalanced or resistant pony will make a hollow outline.

OVER-FACING Asking a pony (or rider) to tackle a difficult or high jump they are not ready for.

A pole on the ground underneath the front of a jump helps the pony judge an accurate take off by giving him a **groundline**.

OXER A spread fence using two sets of wings, where the top front pole is lower than the top back one.

PARALLEL A spread fence using two sets of wings, where the top front and back poles are at the same height.

PLACING POLE In schooling, a pole laid on the ground at a set distance from a fence (usually one non-jumping stride, or a bounce distance, away) to help the pony judge his take-off.

PUISSANCE A knock-out show jumping class involving five jumps. One is a large spread and one a large upright, usually a wall, and these are raised each round. The winners are the last horse and rider to go clear.

REFUSAL When the pony stops in front of an obstacle.

RELATED DISTANCE Set number of strides used by a course-builder between two fences.

RUN-OUT When a pony runs by the side of an obstacle.

SCHEDULE A programme listing the classes to be held at a show.

SCHOOL-MASTER An experienced horse or pony, ideal for a novice rider.

SPREAD A fence that has depth as well as height.

STAIRCASE FENCE A spread fence using three sets of wings, where the first pole is at the lowest height, the middle one higher and the back pole the highest. Also called a 'triple bar'.

STEADYING POLE A pole laid on the ground on the landing side of the jump, usually one or more strides after the fence. Used to steady rushing ponies and encourage a balanced get-away.

STILE An especially narrow upright, often built from rustic or white poles.

TAKE-OFF POLE Pole placed on the ground immediately in front of a fence to help a pony judge his take-off spot.

TAKE YOUR OWN LINE Show jumping class where each fence is given points according to its difficulty. Riders can choose which fences they attempt to clear within the time allowed. The one with the most points is the winner.

TIGER TRAP Type of timber cross-country fence, shaped like an upside-down V. Sometimes built over a ditch.

TRACK The route a rider chooses to take between the fences in a show jumping round.

TRAKEHNER Cross-country fence with a single log or timber pole over a ditch. Can be either straight or off-set at an angle.

TREBLE A combination fence made up of three elements.

UPRIGHT A fence with no depth. Sometimes called a 'vertical'.

WINGS Stands used to support the poles, planks or fillers when building show jumps.

A **tiger trap** is included in most novice cross-country courses. It may have a ditch underneath too.

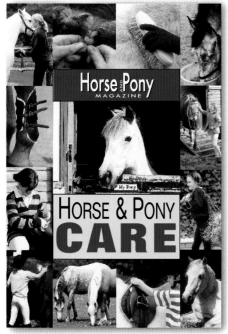
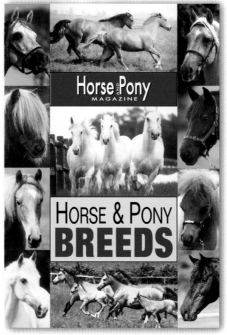
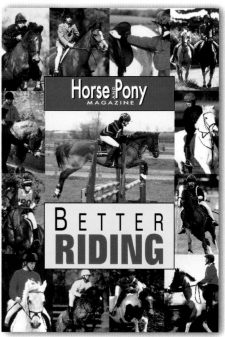
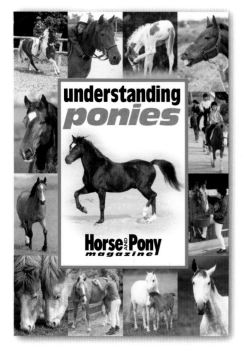
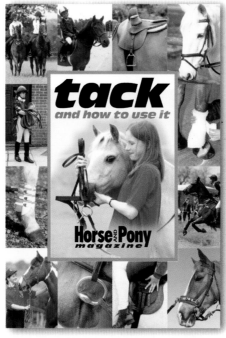